HOLIDAY
CELEBRATIONS
COOKBOOK

HOLIDAY CELEBRATIONS COOKBOOK

Recipes for Your Merry Occasions

Written and Compiled by

Rachel Quillin

BARBOUR
PUBLISHING

ISBN 1-58660-993-9

Cover image © Comstock

Scripture quotations are taken from the King James Version of the Bible.

Published by Barbour Publishing, Inc., P.O. Box 719, Uhrichsville, Ohio 44683
www.barbourbooks.com

Our mission is to publish and distribute inspirational products offering exceptional value and biblical encouragement to the masses.

Member of the
Evangelical Christian
Publishers Association

Printed in the United States of America.
5 4 3 2

TABLE OF CONTENTS

INTRODUCTION

On the twenty-fifth of June, my husband kindly pointed out that we have six months remaining until Christmas. It's like that on the twenty-fifth of each month, and being the "plan ahead" kind of person that I am, I thank him for the reminder and let him know that I'll soon begin my shopping.

Still it seems that no matter how good my intentions are, I find myself scrambling around at the last minute trying to organize shopping, wrapping, decorating, and, yes, even cooking. It leaves me very little time to reflect on why I'm even doing all of this celebrating.

I've often thought how nice it would be to have a collection of recipes at my fingertips—one that would include easy, yet tasty, recipes I could prepare for my family during the mad rush of the holidays, as well as interesting and delicious recipes for special occasions.

Holiday Celebrations is just that collection. It includes breakfast and dinner dishes and everything in between. You will find traditional holiday recipes as well as some fun new dishes to try. I hope you enjoy these recipes and that you will find your holiday meal and party planning go more smoothly as you use this handy cookbook.

God bless and Merry Christmas!

RACHEL QUILLIN

APPETIZERS

At a dinner party, one should eat wisely
but not too well and talk well but not too wisely.

W. SOMERSET MAUGHAM

CRAB DIP

2 8-ounce packages cream cheese, softened
1 jar cocktail sauce
2 cans crabmeat, drained
Lemon slices
Choice of crackers

Mix crabmeat and cocktail sauce in a bowl; set aside. Spread softened cream cheese over a large plate. Pour crab mixture over the cream cheese and garnish with sliced lemons. Serve with crackers.

HOLIDAY SPINACH AND ARTICHOKE DIP

1 pound sour cream
1 package ranch dip mix
1 14-ounce can artichokes, drained and chopped
2 10-ounce packages frozen chopped spinach,
    thawed and well drained
2 1-ounce jars diced pimientos, rinsed and drained
2 round loaves sourdough bread

Mix together the sour cream, ranch dip mix, artichokes, spinach, and pimientos; refrigerate for 1 hour. Cut top off bread and clean out the inside, being careful not to tear open. Save filling; cut up and toast for dippers. Spoon mix into hollowed bread. Bake at 400° for 20–25 minutes. Cover with foil if browning too much. Serve hot or cold.

SPINACH DIP

2 10-ounce packages frozen chopped spinach,
    thawed and drained
1 4-ounce package blue cheese, crumbled
1 8-ounce can sliced water chestnuts
$\frac{1}{2}$ cup chopped celery
$\frac{3}{4}$ cup chopped red pepper
$\frac{1}{2}$ cup chopped green onion
$\frac{1}{2}$ .65-ounce package garlic dressing mix
2 cups sour cream
1 cup mayonnaise
1 loaf whole pumpernickel bread

In a large bowl, combine the spinach and blue cheese. Stir in the water chestnuts, celery, red pepper, green onion, and garlic dressing mix. In a separate bowl, combine the sour cream and mayonnaise. Slowly stir sour cream mixture into spinach mixture until the ingredients are easy to spread. Cut top off bread and clean out the inside, being careful not to tear open. Save the filling for dippers. Spoon mix into hollowed bread.

TACO DIP

1 pound ground beef
1 can refried beans
1 small can chopped green chilies
1 14–16-ounce jar taco sauce
10 ounces or more cheddar cheese, shredded
Salt and pepper to taste
Tostada chips

Brown hamburger and season with salt and pepper; drain. Add the remaining ingredients. Heat until the cheese melts, stirring occasionally. Serve with Tostada chips. Works well when made and served in a Crock-Pot.

CHEESE BALL

2 8-ounce packages cream cheese, softened
4 ounces chopped dried beef
Dash of garlic salt
1 small onion, minced
Dash of Worcestershire sauce
Snack crackers

Mix cream cheese, half of the dried beef, garlic salt, onion, and Worcestershire sauce. Form into 1 large ball or 2 smaller balls. Refrigerate for about 1 hour. Roll in remaining dried beef. Serve with snack crackers

CHEESE BALL

2 8-ounce packages
cream cheese, softened
1 bunch green onions,
chopped (about 4)
1 small can chopped
black olives

1 small can prepared ham,
crumbled with broth
1 cup chopped pecans
1 10-ounce package shredded
medium cheddar cheese
Snack crackers

In a medium-sized bowl, combine cream cheese, onions, olives, and ham. Add about half of the chopped pecans and cheddar cheese. Mix well. Form 2 balls. Roll cheese balls in remaining pecans and cheddar cheese until balls are covered. Chill and serve with snack crackers.

CREAM CHEESE LOG WITH DRIED BEEF

1 8-ounce container
reduced-fat, soft style
cream cheese at room
temperature
$^1/_2$ cup reduced-fat mayonnaise
1 teaspoon drained prepared
horseradish
$^1/_2$ cup Swiss cheese, shredded

2 ounces finely chopped
dried beef
1 tablespoon canned
pimientos, drained and
chopped
$^1/_2$ cup finely chopped chives
or green onion tops
Melba toast slices

In a small bowl, using an electric mixer, beat the cream cheese, mayonnaise, and horseradish until creamy. Stir in Swiss cheese, dried beef, and pimientos. Form into an 8-inch log. Wrap log in plastic wrap and refrigerate for at least 2 hours. Spread the chives or onion tops on waxed paper. Unwrap the log and carefully roll it in the chives, coating it completely. Rewrap in plastic wrap and refrigerate until time to serve. Serve with Melba toast slices.

MINI SAUSAGE BISCUITS

1 tube refrigerated buttermilk biscuits
1 tablespoon butter, melted
1 8-ounce package Brown' N Serve sausage links
4½ teaspoons grated Parmesan cheese
1 teaspoon dried oregano

On a floured surface, roll biscuits into 4-inch circles. Brush each circle with melted butter. Place one sausage link in the center of each biscuit and sprinkle with Parmesan cheese and oregano; roll up. Cut each biscuit widthwise into four pieces. Fasten each with a toothpick. Place biscuits on ungreased cookie sheets and bake at 375° for 8–10 minutes or until golden brown.

NUTTY CHICKEN PUFFS

1½ cups cooked chicken, finely chopped
⅓ cup toasted almonds, chopped
1 cup chicken broth
½ cup vegetable oil
2 teaspoons Worcestershire sauce
1 tablespoon dried parsley flakes
1 teaspoon seasoned salt
½–1 teaspoon celery seed
⅛ teaspoon cayenne pepper
1 cup flour
4 eggs

Mix chicken and almonds; set aside. In a large saucepan, mix chicken broth, vegetable oil, Worcestershire sauce, parsley, seasoned salt, celery seed, and cayenne pepper. Bring mixture to a boil. Add flour, stirring until a smooth ball forms. Remove from heat for 5 minutes. Add eggs one at a time; beat well after each addition. Beat until smooth. Stir in chicken mixture. Drop by heaping teaspoonfuls onto greased baking sheets. Bake at 450° for 12–14 minutes or until golden brown. Serve warm.

PARTY HAM ROLLS

1 package prepared biscuits
½ cup margarine
½ tablespoon poppy seeds
½ teaspoon Worcestershire sauce
½ tablespoon mustard
½ tablespoon onion flakes or minced onion
Baked and sliced ham
Swiss or mozzarella cheese, shredded

Melt margarine; add poppy seeds, Worcestershire sauce, mustard, and onion; set aside. Top biscuits with ham. Pour margarine mixture over biscuits, sprinkle with cheese, and let set overnight. Bake 15–20 minutes at 350°, or until cheese melts.

HOLIDAY HAM BALLS

3 cups buttermilk baking mix
10½ cups smoked ham, finely chopped
4 cups sharp cheddar cheese, shredded
½ cup Parmesan cheese
2 teaspoons parsley flakes
2 teaspoons spicy brown mustard
⅔ teaspoon milk

Lightly grease a 15½ x 10½-inch jellyroll pan. Mix all ingredients well. Shape mixture into 1-inch balls. Place about 2 inches apart in pan. Bake at 350° for 20–25 minutes or until brown. Remove from pan and serve warm.

CRANBERRY ORANGE CRESCENTS

1 8-ounce can refrigerated crescent rolls
1/3 cup finely chopped cranberries
2 tablespoons cracker crumbs
1 teaspoon grated orange peel
1 teaspoon sugar

Separate dough into 8 triangles. Combine all other ingredients and spread evenly over triangles. Roll crescents and bake as directed on package label.

CHRISTMAS CHEESE SCONES

2 cups flour
2 teaspoons baking powder
1/2 teaspoon salt
Pinch cayenne pepper
2 ounces butter
3 ounces cheese, shredded
Milk (to create a fairly firm dough)

Mix flour, baking powder, salt, and pepper. Cut in the butter; mix in just enough milk to incorporate. On a floured surface, roll dough to 1/2-inch thick. Cut into rounds and place on greased cookie sheet. Brush tops with milk and sprinkle with grated cheese. Cook at 400° for 10 minutes. Cool on a wire rack.

PIZZA BREAD

Frozen bread dough
Pizza sauce
Sandwich pepperoni
Provolone or mozzarella cheese

Let frozen dough rise in bread pans overnight. Preheat oven to 375°. Roll out dough and spread sauce to within 1 inch of the sides. Layer pepperoni and cheese on top of sauce. Roll dough lengthwise and fold in the ends to seal. Place on a cookie sheet and bake for about 30 minutes. If you like, you may spread melted butter on baked roll and sprinkle with Parmesan cheese.

HOLIDAY SNACK CRACKERS

1 package ranch dressing dry mix
$3/4$–1 cup salad oil or olive oil
$1/2$–1 teaspoon dill weed
$1/4$–$1/2$ teaspoon garlic powder
$1/4$–$1/2$ teaspoon lemon pepper seasoning
16 ounces plain oyster crackers

Combine ranch dressing mix and oil; add dill weed, garlic powder, and lemon pepper. Pour over crackers; stir well to coat. Place in warm oven for 20 minutes. Stir well halfway through. Store in airtight container.

PUMPKIN PIE SPICED NUTS

1 egg white
1 teaspoon water
24 ounces salted, mixed nuts
1 cup sugar
1 tablespoon Homemade Pumpkin Pie Spice
   (Combine 4 teaspoons ground cinnamon,
   2 teaspoons ground ginger, 1 teaspoon ground
   cloves, and 1/2 teaspoon nutmeg. Store in a
   spice bottle.)

In a large bowl, beat together the egg white and water. Add nuts and toss to coat. Combine sugar and one tablespoon of the spice. Sprinkle over the nuts and toss to coat. In a 15x10x1-inch baking pan, spread nuts in a single layer. Bake at 350° for 20 minutes. Allow to cool slightly before transferring to waxed paper for complete cooling. Break into clumps to serve.

CARAMEL CORN

6 quarts popped corn
1 cup butter
2 cups brown sugar
1 cup dark Karo syrup
1 teaspoon salt
1 teaspoon vanilla extract
½ teaspoon baking soda

Melt butter; stir in brown sugar, Karo, and salt. Boil 5 minutes. Do not stir. Remove from heat. Stir in vanilla and baking soda. Pour over popped corn and stir. Be sure all corn gets coated. Bake at 250° for 1 hour. Stir every 15 minutes.

SAUERKRAUT BALLS

1 medium onion, ground
1½ cups ham
½ clove garlic
1 tablespoon parsley
5 tablespoons butter
5 tablespoons flour

½ cup beef broth
3 cups ground sauerkraut
Breadcrumbs
1 egg
Cooking oil

Brown onion, ham, garlic, and parsley in butter. Add flour, broth, and sauerkraut. Cook until thick and allow to cool. Form into balls. Roll balls in breadcrumbs, then egg, then breadcrumbs again. Deep fry in cooking oil.

STUFFED MUSHROOMS

1½ pounds medium mushrooms (about 30)
½ pound sausage
½ cup mozzarella cheese, shredded
¼ cup seasoned breadcrumbs

Remove stems from mushrooms; chop and set aside. In a large skillet over medium heat, brown sausage. Remove sausage and drain all but 2 tablespoons of drippings. In hot drippings over medium heat, cook stems until tender, about 10 minutes. Remove skillet from heat; stir in sausage, cheese, and crumbs. Fill mushroom caps with sausage mixture and place in casserole dish. Bake at 450° for 15 minutes.

VEGGIE CHRISTMAS TREES
(Makes 2 trees)

2 8-ounce tubes refrigerated crescent rolls
1 8-ounce package cream cheese, softened
½ cup sour cream
1 teaspoon dried dill weed
⅛ teaspoon garlic powder
3 cups finely chopped assorted vegetables (broccoli, carrots, bell peppers, etc.)

Remove dough from tubes. Separate two rolled sections. Do not unroll. Cut each section into 8 slices. There should be 16 slices per tube. Arrange slices cut side down to resemble a Christmas tree on an ungreased cookie sheet. (1 slice for top; two slices just below, etc., until you have 5 rows. The remaining slice should be used for the trunk.) Repeat directions to form second tree. Refrigerate one tree and bake the other at 375° for 11–13 minutes or until golden brown. Cool one minute before removing to wire rack to cool further. Repeat with second tree. Place each tree on serving platter and set aside. Mix cream cheese, sour cream, dill, and garlic powder; blend until smooth. Spread mixture over trees and sprinkle with assorted vegetable pieces. Refrigerate until serving.

CHESTNUT HORS D'OEUVRES

    3 cans whole water chestnuts
    1 pound sliced bacon
    1½ cups ketchup
    1½ cups brown sugar
    1 teaspoon Worcestershire sauce

Drain water chestnuts. Cut bacon slices into 3 sections. Wrap bacon around chestnuts and secure with a toothpick. Bake at 350° for 30 minutes. Drain excess fat. Meanwhile, mix ketchup, brown sugar, and Worcestershire sauce together. Pour over chestnuts and bake for 30 minutes more.

FRESH CRANBERRY SAUCE

4 cups fresh cranberries   2 cups granulated sugar
2 cups water

Cook cranberries in water 5–10 minutes or until all skins pop open. Strain through fine sieve to remove skins and seeds, pressing pulp through with juice. Stir sugar into pulp; boil for 3 minutes. Refrigerate.

HEALTHY HOLIDAY QUESADILLAS

1 8-ounce container nonfat cream cheese
¼ teaspoon garlic powder
¼ teaspoon pepper
8 8-inch flour tortillas
1 9-ounce package frozen spinach, thawed and
   squeezed dry
1 medium red bell pepper, finely chopped
1 cup feta cheese, crumbled

Combine cream cheese, garlic powder, and pepper; blend well. Spread 2 tablespoons of this mixture on each tortilla. Sprinkle two tablespoons of each of the remaining ingredients on half of each tortilla. Fold each tortilla in half. Place 2 tortillas in a hot, large nonstick skillet. Cook tortillas over medium-high heat until golden brown on each side. Place quesadillas on a plate, cover with foil, and repeat directions with remaining tortillas. Cut quesadillas into 4 wedges each. Serve immediately.

CARAMEL APPLE FONDUE

1 14-ounce package caramels
⅓ cup milk
¼ cup margarine
½ teaspoon cinnamon
3 cups apple cubes

In a fondue pot or medium saucepan, mix all ingredients except apples. Heat over low heat until caramels are melted. Stir often. Serve in fondue pot or serving bowl. Dip apples or other dippers (such as pear cubes, pineapple chunks, banana slices, or angel food cake) into caramel mixture using fondue forks or wooden skewers.

PEPPERONI ROLLS

1 8-ounce package
   cream cheese, softened
1 cup cheddar cheese,
   shredded
½ cup sliced ripe olives
2 tablespoons chopped fresh
   oregano or 2 teaspoons dried

2 tablespoons sliced
   green onion
½ teaspoon garlic powder
4 10-inch flour tortillas
1 package giant sliced
   pepperoni

Combine cheeses, olives, oregano, onion, and garlic powder in a medium-sized mixing bowl. Spread ½ cup of the mixture on each tortilla. Place 5 slices of pepperoni down the middle of each tortilla. Roll tortillas up jellyroll style. Wrap each tortilla in plastic wrap and refrigerate at least 2 hours. When ready to serve, cut each tortilla into 12 slices.

DILLY CHEESE CUBES

1 loaf French bread, unsliced
½ cup butter
4 cups cheddar cheese,
   shredded
2 teaspoons dried dill weed

1 teaspoon Worcestershire
   sauce
1 tablespoon grated onion
2 eggs, slightly beaten

Remove crust from bread. Cut bread into 1-inch cubes and set aside. Combine butter and cheese in a medium saucepan. Stir over low heat until mixture is melted. Add dill weed, Worcestershire sauce, and onion. Beat in eggs. Remove from heat. Using a fork, dip each bread cube into hot cheese mixture, being sure to coat on all sides. Shake off excess sauce. Place coated cubes on an ungreased baking sheet. Refrigerate 1–2 days or freeze. Once frozen, bread cubes may be stored in airtight containers in the freezer for up to 6 months. To serve, bake refrigerated cubes at 350° for 10 minutes; frozen cubes need to be baked for 15 minutes. Serve hot.

SWEET BACON BITES

½ pound bacon   Cinnamon to taste
½ cup brown sugar

Cut each slice of bacon in half. Mix brown sugar and cinnamon and coat each slice of bacon. Bake at 350° for 15–20 minutes or until bacon is crisp and sugar mixture bubbles. During baking, occasionally remove some of the fat.

MINI BEEF QUICHES

¼ pound ground beef
¼ teaspoon garlic powder
⅛ teaspoon pepper
1 cup biscuit mix
¼ cup cornmeal
¼ cup cold butter
2–3 tablespoons
    boiling water
1 egg
½ cup half-and-half
1 tablespoon chopped
    green onion
1 tablespoon chopped
    red bell pepper
¼ teaspoon salt
¼ teaspoon cayenne pepper
½ cup cheddar cheese,
    finely shredded

In a saucepan over medium heat, brown beef, garlic powder, and pepper. Drain and set aside. Combine biscuit mix and cornmeal in a bowl. Cut the butter into the cornmeal mixture. Add just enough water to mixture to form soft dough. Press into the bottom and sides of greased mini muffin cups. Add a teaspoonful of the beef mixture to each shell. In a separate bowl, mix egg, half-and-half, onion, red pepper, salt, and cayenne pepper. Pour over the beef. Sprinkle with cheese. Bake at 375° for 20 minutes or until a fork inserted at the center comes out clean.

TUNA CHEESE SPREAD

1 8-ounce package cream cheese, softened
1 6-ounce can tuna, drained and flaked
$\frac{1}{2}$ cup green onions, finely sliced
$\frac{1}{4}$ cup mayonnaise
1 tablespoon lemon juice
$\frac{3}{4}$ teaspoon curry powder
Dash salt
Bread or crackers

Mix first seven ingredients well. Spread on bread slices. Top with another slice of bread and cut sandwiches into quarters. Other options include spreading on crackers or carrot and celery sticks.

SPICY PARTY MIX

10 cups Crispix or
   Chex cereal
2 cups salted peanuts
1½ cups pretzel sticks
½ cup sesame seeds, toasted
½ cup vegetable oil

2 tablespoons lemon juice
1 tablespoon chili powder
1 tablespoon curry powder
1 teaspoon garlic salt
1 teaspoon onion salt
½ teaspoon ground cumin

In a large bowl, mix cereal, peanuts, pretzel sticks, and sesame seeds. Set aside. Combine remaining ingredients in a saucepan and bring to a boil. Pour over cereal mixture and stir to coat. Spread over the bottom of a greased 15x10x1-inch baking pan. Bake at 250° for 10 minutes or until golden. Stir once during baking. Cool completely before serving. Should be stored in an airtight container to maintain freshness.

BEVERAGES

But whosoever drinketh of the water that
I shall give him shall never thirst;
but the water that I shall give him shall be in him
a well of water springing up into everlasting life.

JOHN 4:14

ENGLISH WASSAIL

3 oranges
Whole cloves
3 quarts apple cider
2 3-inch cinnamon sticks

½ teaspoon nutmeg
½ cup honey
⅓ cup lemon juice
2 teaspoons lemon rind
5 cups pineapple juice

Stud oranges with cloves about ½-inch apart. Place in baking pan with a little water. Bake slowly for 30 minutes. Heat cider and cinnamon sticks in large saucepan. Bring to a boil. Simmer, covered, for 5 minutes. Add remaining ingredients and simmer, uncovered, 5 minutes more. Pour into a punchbowl; float spiced oranges on top. Use cinnamon sticks for stirring. May also use slow cooker to keep hot.

WASSAIL

1 gallon apple cider
2 quarts orange juice
1 cup granulated sugar

½ teaspoon salt
3 3-inch cinnamon sticks
½ teaspoon whole cloves

Combine ingredients in a pan. Simmer for three hours over low heat. Strain. Serve hot.

1979 CRANBERRY TEA

1 pound cranberries or 1 quart cranberry juice
3 quarts water, divided
1 cup hot cinnamon candy
½ cup lemon juice
2 cups sugar
10 whole cloves

Cook cranberries in 1 quart water until tender; strain and use juice. Add remaining 2 quarts water and rest of ingredients; heat and serve. May use a slow cooker on low to keep tea warm.

ORANGE SPICED TEA

1 cup powdered orange drink mix
1 heaping cup lemon instant tea, unsweetened
3 cups sugar or sugar substitute
1 teaspoon cinnamon
½ teaspoon nutmeg or ground cloves

Mix all ingredients together. Put 3 heaping teaspoons of mix to one medium mug of boiling water. Use more or less to suit your taste.

HOT SPICED TEA

Juice of three lemons
Juice of three oranges
½ cup blended tea
1 teaspoon ground cinnamon

1 teaspoon nutmeg
3 cups sugar
1 teaspoon whole cloves
1 quart water

Put spices into a cloth bag, then place ingredients in a porcelain kettle and let steep for 3 hours. Strain into jars. When ready to use, add enough water to make 1 gallon tea. Reheat as any other spiced tea.

DONNA'S CHRISTMAS PUNCH

1 12-ounce can frozen concentrated grape juice,
   thawed and undiluted
½ 12-ounce can frozen cranberry cocktail juice
   concentrate, thawed and undiluted
2 cups orange juice
1 2-liter bottle lemon-lime soda
Orange or lemon slices

Mix all ingredients together in punchbowl and garnish with orange or lime slices. Add an ice ring or crushed ice. Depending upon the number of people at your holiday celebration, you may want to double the recipe.

CHRISTMAS PUNCH

3 teaspoons whole cloves
3 teaspoons ground allspice
1 whole nutmeg
Crushed cinnamon sticks (about 3 inches each)
½ cup brown sugar, firmly packed
4 cups orange juice
6 cups cranberry juice
1 cup water
6 ounces frozen lemonade concentrate, thawed
    and undiluted

Place spices in a spice bag. Put the bag in a saucepan and add the other ingredients. Bring to a boil, stirring often. Cover and reduce heat, letting the mixture simmer for 30 minutes.

TROPICAL FRUIT PUNCH

1 cup sugar
1 cup water
3 cups grapefruit juice
3 cups orange juice
3 cups pineapple juice
½ cup lemon juice
½ cup lime juice
1 2-liter bottle ginger ale,
    chilled

Combine sugar and water in a saucepan. Bring to a boil. Boil for 2 minutes, stirring constantly. Remove from heat and allow to cool. Pour into a punchbowl and add juices. Cover and refrigerate until ready to serve. Add ginger ale immediately before serving.

ANGEL FROST PUNCH

2 10-ounce packages frozen sliced strawberries
2 6-ounce cans frozen pink lemonade concentrate,
    undiluted
2 cups water
1 quart vanilla ice cream
2 cups lemon-lime soda, chilled

Combine 1 package strawberries, 1 can lemonade concentrate, 1 cup water, and half of the ice cream in blender. Blend until thick and smooth. Pour into a punchbowl. Repeat the process with remaining strawberries, lemonade concentrate, water, and ice cream. Carefully pour soda down the side of the punchbowl. Gently stir to mix.

CRANBERRY PUNCH

1 quart cranberry juice
$\frac{1}{3}$ cup sugar
4 1-inch cinnamon sticks
2 cups lemon-lime soda

Combine cranberry juice, sugar, and cinnamon sticks in a saucepan. Simmer for 15 minutes. Remove from heat. Remove cinnamon sticks; cover and chill. At serving time add the soda.

CHERRY SPARKLE PUNCH

1½ ounces cherry-flavored powdered drink mix
1 cup sugar
2 cups milk
1 quart vanilla ice cream
1 quart lemon-lime soda

Combine first two ingredients; dissolve with milk. Add ice cream in small scoops. Slowly add soda. Stir slightly.

HOT FRUIT PUNCH

1 6-ounce can frozen orange juice concentrate,
    undiluted
10 cups water
1 teaspoon vanilla extract
1 6-ounce can frozen lemonade concentrate,
    undiluted
1½ cups sugar
1 teaspoon almond extract

Combine all ingredients. Heat slowly, but do not bring to a boil.

PEPPERMINT PUNCH

1 6-ounce can frozen orange juice concentrate,
    thawed and undiluted
1 6-ounce can frozen limeade concentrate,
    thawed and undiluted
1 6-ounce can frozen lemonade concentrate,
    thawed and undiluted
1 tray ice cubes
1 46-ounce can pineapple juice
1 quart peppermint ice cream
1 package frozen strawberries
1 quart ginger ale, well chilled

Combine all concentrates. Add ice cubes and pineapple juice. Mix thoroughly and chill. Just before serving, blend in ice cream, using an electric mixer. Stir in strawberries. Add ginger ale and stir thoroughly.

STRAWBERRY PUNCH

1 quart strawberry sherbet
1 quart lemon-lime soda
1 quart ginger ale
1 small can frozen pink lemonade concentrate,
    thawed and undiluted

Blend all ingredients together and serve.

ORANGE SLUSH PUNCH

2 cups sugar
6 cups water
4 bananas, mashed
½ cup lemon juice
2 12-ounce cans frozen orange juice concentrate,
    thawed and undiluted
1 46-ounce can pineapple juice
1 2-liter bottle lemon-lime soda, chilled

Combine sugar and water in a Dutch oven; cook over high heat, stirring often, until sugar dissolves. Let cool. Stir in bananas, lemon juice, orange juice concentrate, and pineapple juice. Freeze until firm. Remove from freezer 2 hours before serving. Break frozen mixture into large pieces and place in punchbowl. Add soda and stir gently.

ICY HOLIDAY PUNCH

1 6-ounce package cherry gelatin
¾ cup sugar
2 cups boiling water
1 46-ounce can pineapple juice
6 cups cold water
1 2-liter bottle ginger ale, chilled

Dissolve gelatin and sugar in boiling water. Stir in pineapple juice and cold water. Cover and freeze overnight. Allow to thaw 2 hours before serving. Just before serving, pour into a punch-bowl and stir in chilled ginger ale.

CHRISTMAS SLUSH

2 6-ounce cans frozen orange juice concentrate,
    thawed and undiluted
4½ cups water
2 46-ounce cans fruit punch
1 46-ounce can pineapple juice, unsweetened
1 48-ounce bottle cranapple juice
1 2-liter bottle ginger ale, chilled

Combine orange juice concentrate and water; mix well. Add remaining juices. Freeze in large container, but stir occasionally. 3½ hours before serving time, remove the mixture from the freezer. Continue to stir occasionally as the mixture thaws. Immediately before serving, add the ginger ale. Stir to mix thoroughly.

ORANGE SLUSH

2 cups cold water
2 cups granulated sugar
1 6-ounce can frozen orange juice concentrate,
    undiluted
Ginger ale

In a saucepan, mix sugar and water. Bring to a boil and cook for 2 minutes. Remove from heat and add orange juice concentrate. Freeze. When ready to serve, spoon into glasses. Pour ginger ale over slush mixture.

FRUIT SLUSH WITH APRICOTS

1 12-ounce can frozen orange juice concentrate,
    thawed and undiluted
6 bananas
1 2½-pound can apricots
1 2-pound can crushed pineapple
1 jar maraschino cherries or 1 16-ounce package
    strawberries, juice included

Mix juice, bananas, and apricots in blender. Add remaining
ingredients and stir in large bowl. Put into 9-ounce clear plastic
cups and freeze. Thaw 15–30 seconds in microwave to serve.
Adjust ingredients and amounts according to your needs.

CRANBERRY SHRUB

1 48-ounce bottle cranberry juice
2 46-ounce cans pineapple juice
Lemon, orange, or pineapple sherbet

Mix juices thoroughly. Pour into individual glasses and add a
scoop of sherbet. Serve immediately. To make into a punch, add
1 quart lemon-lime soda to every gallon of shrub.

HOT CHOCOLATE

1 1-pound can powdered chocolate drink mix
1 pound sugar
1 8-quart box confectioners' sugar
1 3–6-ounce jar powdered creamer

Sift all ingredients together. Store in airtight container. For 1 mug of hot chocolate, add 4 heaping teaspoons of mixture to 1 cup boiling water.

MEXICAN COFFEE

$\frac{1}{2}$ cup packed brown sugar
6 cups warm water
$\frac{1}{2}$ cup regular grind coffee
$\frac{1}{2}$ ounce unsweetened chocolate
2 tablespoons ground cinnamon
1 tablespoon chamomile tea
2 whole cloves
$\frac{1}{2}$ teaspoon vanilla extract

In a 3-quart saucepan, heat brown sugar until melted. Stir constantly to avoid scorching. Remove from heat and slowly stir in water. Add coffee, chocolate, cinnamon, tea, and cloves. Stir to mix thoroughly. Heat to boiling. Reduce heat and simmer for 15 minutes. Stir in vanilla. Strain coffee through 2 pieces of cheesecloth.

SPICED CIDER

2 quarts apple cider
$1/2$ cup packed brown sugar
3 3-inch cinnamon sticks
$1/2$–1 teaspoon ground allspice
$1/8$ teaspoon salt
$1/8$ teaspoon ground nutmeg

In a large saucepan, combine all ingredients. Bring to a boil over high heat. Reduce heat; simmer, covered, for 20 minutes. Discard cinnamon sticks. If desired, additional cinnamon sticks may be used as garnish or stirrers.

SPICED APRICOT CIDER

2 12-ounce cans apricot nectar
2 cups water
$1/4$ cup lemon juice
$1/4$ cup sugar
2 whole cloves
2 3-inch cinnamon sticks

Combine all ingredients in a slow cooker and mix well. Cook covered for 2 hours. Remove cloves and cinnamon sticks. Serve hot.

GOLDEN PUNCH

1 2-liter bottle lemon-lime soda
1 46-ounce can unsweetened pineapple juice
1 12-ounce can frozen lemonade, diluted with 3⅓
   cans water
½ cup sugar

Chill soda, juice, and lemonade. Mix all in a punchbowl. Add sugar. Stir until dissolved.

STEAMING HOT HOLIDAY PUNCH

3 cups apple juice
3 cups orange juice
6 cups cranberry juice cocktail
¾ cup maple syrup
2 teaspoons confectioners' sugar
½ teaspoon ground cinnamon
¾ teaspoon ground cloves
¾ teaspoon ground nutmeg
Cinnamon sticks (optional)

Combine all ingredients except cinnamon sticks in a heavy pan. Bring to boil. Reduce to simmer for a few minutes. Keep warm in a slow cooker if desired. Cinnamon sticks may be used as stirrers.

CRANBERRY CIDER PUNCH

2 liters cranberry ginger ale, chilled
2 liters apple cider, chilled
3 limes
1 can frozen raspberry juice concentrate (optional)

Combine ginger ale and cider in a punchbowl. Squeeze juice from two of the limes. Stir into punch. If desired, add the raspberry juice concentrate. Refrigerate until serving time. When ready to serve, thinly slice remaining lime. Float lime slices on top of punch.

HOT CRANBERRY BEVERAGE

3 quarts water
3 cups fresh cranberries
3 lemons, sliced
3 oranges, sliced
12 whole cloves
3 2-inch cinnamon sticks
2 cups honey
1 teaspoon ground nutmeg

In a Dutch oven, mix water, cranberries, lemons, and oranges. Bring to a boil. Allow to cook until cranberry skins break open. Strain mixture. Place cloves and cinnamon sticks in a spice bag. Add to the Dutch oven. Add honey and nutmeg to Dutch oven. Cook over medium heat for 10 minutes. Stir occasionally. Remove spice bag and serve beverage immediately.

GRAPE SMOOTHIES

1 pint vanilla ice cream, softened
1 6-ounce can frozen grape juice concentrate,
    undiluted
1½ cups milk

Combine all ingredients in a blender. Cover and blend until smooth. Serve at once.

GOLDEN SMOOTHIES

1½ cups orange juice
1 8-ounce container peach yogurt
1 5½-ounce can apricot nectar
1 teaspoon honey
Orange slices and maraschino cherries (optional)

Combine orange juice, yogurt, nectar, and honey in a blender. Cover and blend until smooth. Pour into individual serving glasses. If desired, use orange slices and cherries as garnishes.

BREADS

And Jesus said unto them, I am the bread of life:
he that cometh to me shall never hunger;
and he that believeth on me shall never thirst.

JOHN 6:35

REFRIGERATOR ROLLS

2 cups boiling water
1½ cups sugar
1 tablespoon salt
½ cup shortening
2 scant tablespoons active dry yeast (2 packages)
1 cup lukewarm water
1 teaspoon sugar
2 eggs, beaten
10–11 cups flour (sapphire is best)

Pour boiling water over 1½ cups sugar. Add salt and shortening. Let cool until lukewarm. Dissolve yeast in lukewarm water. Add 1 teaspoon sugar and the eggs. Mix well and add to first mixture. Beat in flour until dough pulls away from the sides of the bowl. Cover dough with cloth and let rise until doubled. Punch down dough. Form rolls (about golf ball-sized). Place in greased pan and let rise until doubled. Bake at 375° for about 12 minutes.

NOTE: Keep hands greased while forming rolls. For 12 rolls use a 9x13-inch pan. For 8 rolls use a round cake pan. Unused dough may be stored in refrigerator until ready to use.

DINNER ROLLS

4¼–4¾ cups flour
1 package active dry yeast
1 cup milk
⅓ cup sugar

⅓ cup butter
¾ teaspoon salt
2 eggs, beaten

In large mixing bowl, stir together 2 cups of the flour and the yeast. In medium saucepan, heat and stir milk, sugar, butter, and salt until warm (120°) and butter almost melts. Add milk mixture to dry mix along with eggs; mix well using hands. Mix in the remaining flour. Knead in enough to make moderately stiff dough that is smooth and elastic. Shape into ball. Place in lightly greased bowl. Turn once; cover and let rise until double, about 1 hour. Divide dough in half; cover and let rest for 10 minutes. Lightly grease cookie sheets. Shape into desired rolls; cover and let rise in warm place until nearly double, about 30 minutes. Bake at 375° for 12–15 minutes or until golden.

BACON-ONION PAN ROLLS

1 pound frozen bread dough, thawed
¼ cup butter, melted and divided
½ pound sliced bacon, cooked and crumbled
½ cup chopped onion

On a lightly floured board, roll dough to a ¼-inch thickness. Cut rolls using a 2½-inch biscuit cutter. Brush rolls using 3 tablespoons melted butter. Place 1 teaspoon each of bacon and onion on half of each roll. Fold over and pinch to seal. With pinched sides up, place rolls in a greased 9-inch square baking pan, forming 3 rows of 6. Brush tops with remaining butter. Let rise until doubled, about 30 minutes. Bake at 350° for 25–30 minutes or until golden brown.

SOURDOUGH BISCUITS

2 cups biscuit mix
¾ cup plus 2 tablespoons Sourdough Starter (recipe
    follows)

Stir biscuit mix and sourdough starter just until the biscuit mix is
moistened. Turn dough out onto a lightly floured surface. Gently
knead 3–4 times. Roll dough to ½-inch thickness. Cut with a
2-inch biscuit cutter. Place biscuits on lightly greased cookie sheet
with their sides touching. Bake at 400° for 12–14 minutes.

SOURDOUGH STARTER

2 cups all-purpose flour
2 tablespoons sugar

1 package active dry yeast
2½ cups warm water
    (120°–130°)

Combine first 3 ingredients in a medium-sized glass bowl.
Gradually add warm water and mix well. Cover loosely with
plastic wrap. Keep in warm place (85°) for 72 hours. Stir 1–2
times daily.

CINNAMON ROLLS

2 packages active dry yeast
½ cup warm water
1½ cups milk (warm)
½ cup sugar
2 teaspoons salt
2 eggs

½ cup shortening
7–7½ cups flour
8 tablespoons butter, melted
1½ cups brown sugar
3 teaspoons cinnamon

Dissolve yeast in warm water. Mix in milk, sugar, salt, eggs, shortening, and flour. Put into greased bowl and let rise until doubled in size. Punch down dough and divide in half. Mix melted butter, brown sugar, and cinnamon and set aside. Roll half of dough into a rectangle about ¼-inch thick. Brush with half of butter mixture. Roll up like jellyroll. Slice and place in greased pans. Repeat with second half of dough. Let rise. Bake at 350° for 15–20 minutes.

ICING:

1 pound confectioners' sugar
¾ stick softened butter
17 shakes of salt
1 teaspoon vanilla extract
Milk (enough to make icing spreadable)

Stir all ingredients together and spread on warm cinnamon rolls. This icing is also delicious on cutout cookies.

CRANBERRY MUFFINS

FILLING:

1 cup chopped fresh or frozen cranberries

2 tablespoons sugar

MUFFINS:

2 cups flour
$\frac{1}{3}$ cup sugar
2 teaspoons baking powder
$\frac{1}{2}$ teaspoon salt

$\frac{1}{2}$ cup cold butter
$\frac{3}{4}$ cup orange juice
1 egg, slightly beaten

TOPPING:

$\frac{1}{4}$ cup butter, melted

$\frac{1}{4}$ cup sugar

Combine filling ingredients and set aside. In a large bowl, stir together flour, $\frac{1}{3}$ cup sugar, baking powder, and salt. Cut in cold butter until mixture is coarse. Stir in orange juice and egg until mixture is lightly moistened. Gently stir in filling mixture. Spoon batter into greased or paper-lined muffin pans. Bake at 400° for 20–25 minutes or until golden brown. Cool 5 minutes and remove from pan. Spread tops of muffins with melted butter and sprinkle with sugar.

PECAN SWEET ROLL RINGS

2 8-ounce tubes refrigerated
  crescent rolls
4 tablespoons butter, melted
  and divided
1/2 cup chopped pecans

1/4 cup sugar
1 teaspoon ground cinnamon
1/2 teaspoon ground nutmeg
1/2 cup confectioners' sugar
2 tablespoons maple syrup

Separate crescent dough into 8 rectangles. Seal the perforations. Brush rectangles using 2 tablespoons butter. Mix the pecans, sugar, cinnamon, and nutmeg. Sprinkle 1 tablespoon of the pecan mixture over each rectangle. Press lightly into the dough. Roll each rectangle up jellyroll style, starting at the long side. Seal the seams. Twist each roll 2–3 times. Cut six shallow diagonal slits in each roll. Shape each roll into a ring, pinching ends to seal. Place on a greased baking sheet and brush with remaining butter. Bake at 375° for 12–14 minutes or until golden brown. Combine confectioners' sugar and maple syrup until smooth. Drizzle over warm rolls.

PECAN STICKY BUNS

1/2 cup chopped pecans
1 package frozen dinner rolls
1/2 cup butter

1/2 cup sugar
1/2 cup brown sugar
1 teaspoon cinnamon

Grease a Bundt or angel food pan. Sprinkle bottom of pan with chopped nuts and place frozen rolls on top of nuts. In a saucepan melt butter, sugar, brown sugar, and cinnamon. Pour mixture over rolls. Cover rolls and allow to stand overnight. Bake at 350° for 25 minutes.

BUTTERSCOTCH BUNS

½ cup chopped pecans
¼ cup butter, melted
½ cup sugar
1 teaspoon ground cinnamon

1 package refrigerated
  biscuits (10-count)
½ cup butterscotch morsels
⅓ cup evaporated milk

Grease and flour a 9-inch round cake pan; cover the bottom of pan with chopped nuts. Set aside. Melt butter in a small bowl and set aside. In another small bowl combine sugar and cinnamon. Separate biscuits and dip both sides of each biscuit into the melted butter, then into the sugar-cinnamon mixture. Place biscuits on nuts in the pan. Bake at 400° for 10 minutes or until golden brown. In a small saucepan, combine butterscotch morsels with evaporated milk. Heat over medium heat, stirring constantly, until the morsels are melted and the mixture is smooth. Pour mixture over the hot buns.

CINNAMON STICKY BUNS

1 cup packed brown sugar
½ cup corn syrup
½ cup butter
1 cup pecans, coarsely
  chopped

½ cup sugar
¼ cup ground cinnamon
2 17.3-ounce tubes large
  refrigerated biscuits

Mix brown sugar, corn syrup, and butter in a saucepan. Cook until sugar dissolves, stirring constantly. Add pecans to mixture. Spoon into a greased 13x9x2-inch baking pan. In a shallow bowl, mix sugar and cinnamon. Cut each biscuit in half and dip into cinnamon mixture. Bake at 375° for 25–30 minutes or until golden brown. Invert onto a platter and serve.

HOLIDAY BUNS

4 cups warm water
1 cup sugar
1 package active dry yeast
1 egg
3 teaspoons salt

1 cup oil
10 cups flour
1 cup raisins (optional)
2 teaspoons cinnamon
  (optional)

Combine water, sugar, and yeast. Cover and let stand 10 minutes. Mix in egg, salt, oil, and flour, and let rise until doubled. Put into cupcake tins for round rolls. Bake at 350° for 20 minutes.

VARIATION: For raisin bread, add raisins and cinnamon.

BUTTERMILK YEAST BUNS

¼ cup warm water (100°–115°)
1 package active dry yeast
3 cups buttermilk, room
  temperature
½ cup sugar

½ cup butter, melted
2 eggs, beaten
1 teaspoon baking soda
1 teaspoon salt
8 cups all-purpose flour
Additional butter, melted

Pour water into a large mixing bowl. Crumble yeast into water, stirring to dissolve. Add buttermilk and sugar; allow to stand for 15 minutes. Add warm butter and beaten eggs; mix. Sift baking soda and salt with half of the flour. Add soda mixture to liquid mixture. Beat until a smooth batter forms. Add remaining flour. Stir with spoon until dough is no longer sticky. Knead on a floured surface. Place in a large greased bowl. Turn once to be sure the top is greased. Cover and let rise until doubled (about 1 hour). Punch dough down and form into buns (squeeze dough into egg-sized balls). Place on a greased baking sheet and flatten slightly. Let rise until doubled (about 30 minutes). Bake at 400° for 15–20 minutes or until light golden brown. Remove to cooling rack and brush top with melted butter.

BLUEBERRY-ORANGE BREAD

2 tablespoons butter
¼ cup boiling water
1 tablespoon grated
   orange rind
½ cup orange juice
1 egg

1 cup sugar
2 cups all-purpose flour
1 teaspoon baking powder
¼ teaspoon baking soda
½ teaspoon salt
1 cup fresh blueberries

SYRUP:

1 teaspoon grated orange rind
2 tablespoons fresh orange juice
2 tablespoons honey

In a small bowl, combine butter and boiling water. Add grated orange rind and orange juice. Set mixture aside. Beat egg and sugar with a mixer until light and fluffy. Combine the flour, baking powder, soda, and salt; add to egg mixture alternately with orange juice mixture, beginning and ending with flour mixture. Fold in blueberries. Grease and flour a 9x5x3-inch loaf pan and spoon batter into it. Bake at 350° for 55 minutes. Cool bread in pan 10 minutes; remove to wire rack. Combine syrup ingredients, mixing well. Spoon over hot bread; let cool.

GLAZED LEMON BREAD

¾ cup margarine
1½ cups sugar
3 eggs
2¼ cups flour

¼ teaspoon salt
¼ teaspoon baking soda
¾ cup buttermilk
Rind of 2 lemons

GLAZE:

¾ cup sugar

Juice of 2 lemons

Cream together margarine and sugar. Beat in eggs. Mix dry ingredients. Starting with dry mixture, add dry mixture and buttermilk alternately to margarine mixture. Stir in lemon rind. Pour into greased loaf pan. Bake at 350° for 1 hour. Meanwhile mix ¾ cup sugar and lemon juice until sugar dissolves. When bread is done, pierce warm bread with a fork and drizzle glaze over the top.

RAISIN BREAD

1¼ cups sugar
¼ cup cooking oil
2 eggs
6 cups flour

2 teaspoons salt
7 teaspoons baking powder
3½ cups milk
1½ cups raisins

In large bowl, mix sugar, cooking oil, and eggs. Set aside. In a separate bowl mix flour, salt, and baking powder. Alternately stir milk and flour mixture into sugar mixture. Mix well. Blend in raisins. Pour batter into well-greased loaf pans. Let stand 20 minutes. Bake at 350° for 1 hour or until done. Makes 2–3 loaves.

CHUNKY APPLE BREAD

4 eggs
2 cups sugar
½ cup buttermilk
½ cup regular mayonnaise
1 teaspoon vanilla extract
3½ cups all-purpose flour
1 teaspoon baking powder

1 teaspoon ground cinnamon
½ teaspoon baking soda
¼ teaspoon salt
2 medium tart apples,
    peeled and chopped
1 cup raisins
1 cup walnuts, chopped

In a large bowl, mix eggs, sugar, buttermilk, mayonnaise, and vanilla. In a separate bowl, combine the flour, baking powder, cinnamon, baking soda, and salt; add to egg mixture and beat just until combined. Fold in fruits and nuts. Spoon into 2 greased 8x4x2-inch loaf pans. Bake at 375° for 1 hour or until fork inserted at the center comes out clean. Cool for 10 minutes. Remove to wire racks to complete cooling.

JULEKAGE (CHRISTMAS BREAD)

1 cup milk (¾ cup milk and
    ¼ cup water if dry yeast is
    used instead of cake yeast)
2 cakes or packages yeast
½ cup sugar
2 eggs
1 teaspoon salt

6 cardamom seeds, ground
4 cups flour
¼ cup butter
⅔ package candied fruit
Black raisins
White raisins

POWDERED SUGAR FROSTING:
    3 cups powdered sugar
    ⅓ cup soft butter
    1½ teaspoons almond flavoring
    2 tablespoons milk

Scald and cool milk. When milk is lukewarm, dissolve yeast in milk. Mix in sugar, slightly beaten eggs, salt, cardamom, and two cups flour. Melt butter and add to mixture. Mix well. Add remaining flour, but keep dough "sticky." Mix in candied fruit and a good handful each of black and white raisins, packing in as much fruit as the mixture will hold. Knead on floured board until smooth. Put into a greased bowl to rise until doubled in size (2 hours or longer). After dough is risen, cut dough down with a knife while dough is in bowl. Let rise again, about 45 minutes. Divide dough into two parts and pound down. Shape into loaves and let rise to about twice its size again. Bread can be baked in bread pans or formed into round loaves and baked on a greased cookie sheet or in a greased pie pan. Bake at 350° for 30–40 minutes. Bread may be frosted with a powdered sugar frosting while bread is still warm. To make frosting, cream together the sugar and butter. Stir in flavoring and add milk until desired consistency is reached.

PULL-APART CHEESE BREAD

2 packages buttermilk biscuits
3 tablespoons butter
1 teaspoon garlic salt
1 teaspoon Italian seasoning
3/4 cup mozzarella and cheddar cheese, shredded

Melt butter in bottom of bread pan and sprinkle with garlic salt and Italian seasoning. Roll biscuits in butter and seasonings. Bake at 325° for 20–25 minutes. Halfway through, sprinkle cheese on top.

QUICK ONION BREAD

1 1/2 cups biscuit mix
2 tablespoons dried minced
   onion
1/2 cup milk
1/3 cup water
1 egg, lightly beaten
1/2 teaspoon hot pepper sauce
2 tablespoons butter, melted

In a bowl, mix together the first six ingredients. Mixture should be lumpy. Pour mixture into a greased 9-inch pie plate. Drizzle butter over top. Bake at 400° for 18–22 minutes or until knife inserted near center comes out clean. Cool 10 minutes before cutting. Serve warm.

CREAM CHEESE BRAID

1 8-ounce container sour
  cream, scalded
½ cup sugar
½ cup butter, melted
1 teaspoon salt

2 packages active dry yeast
½ cup warm water
4 cups flour
2 eggs, beaten

FILLING:

¼ cup sugar
1 egg, beaten
⅛ teaspoon salt

2 teaspoons vanilla extract
2 8-ounce packages
  cream cheese, softened

GLAZE:

2 cups confectioners' sugar
¼ cup milk

2 teaspoons vanilla extract

Combine sour cream, sugar, butter, and salt. Mix well. Let cool until lukewarm. Meanwhile, dissolve yeast in warm water. Stir water into first mixture. Stir in flour and eggs. Mixture will be soft. Put into bowl and cover tightly. Refrigerate overnight. Divide dough into 4 parts and knead each part 4–5 times on a floured surface. Roll sections into 12x8-inch rectangles. Spread one-fourth of filling over each section. Roll lengthwise as jelly-rolls. Tuck ends under. Place seam side down on greased baking sheets. Let rise until double. Bake at 375° for 15–20 minutes. Mix ingredients for glaze; pour on cool loaves.

HUNGARIAN BUTTER HORNS

4 cups sifted flour
½ teaspoon salt
1 package or cake yeast
1¼ cups butter

1 teaspoon vanilla extract
3 egg yolks, beaten
½ cup sour cream

FILLING:

3 egg whites
¼ cup finely chopped
  walnuts

1 cup granulated sugar
1 teaspoon vanilla extract

Mix flour and salt. Crumble yeast into flour. Cut butter into flour mixture. Add next three ingredients. For filling, beat egg whites until stiff. Add sugar and fold in nuts and vanilla. Dredge board with confectioners' sugar. Divide dough into 6 sections. Cover one section at a time with waxed paper and roll to the size of a pie tin. Spread with filling and cut into 12 wedges. Roll wedges toward center, shaping into crescents. Do not allow to rise. Place crescents on greased cookie sheets and bake at 400° for 10–15 minutes.

PUMPKIN ROLL

3 eggs
1 cup sugar
⅔ cup pumpkin
1 teaspoon lemon juice
¾ cup flour
1 teaspoon baking powder

2 teaspoons cinnamon
1 teaspoon ginger
½ teaspoon nutmeg
½ teaspoon salt
1 cup chopped nuts

FILLING:
1 cup confectioners' sugar, sifted
1 8-ounce package cream cheese, softened
4 tablespoons butter, softened
½ teaspoon vanilla extract

Beat eggs on high speed. Blend in sugar, pumpkin, and lemon juice. Stir in dry ingredients. Spread on a waxed paper-lined cookie sheet. Top with nuts and bake at 375° for 15 minutes. Heavily dust a clean dish towel with confectioners' sugar; peel waxed paper from pumpkin roll and roll it and the towel up together like a cinnamon roll. Allow to cool for 1–1½ hours. Blend the filling ingredients until smooth. Unroll the towel and roll; spread filling evenly over flat surface. Then reroll without the towel. Should resemble a jellyroll.

BREAKFAST
DISHES

All happiness depends on a leisurely breakfast.

JOHN GUNTER

BREAKFAST CASSEROLE

1 pound sausage
6 eggs, beaten
1 teaspoon salt
1 teaspoon dry mustard

1 cup cheese, shredded
1 cup milk
2 slices day-old bread, torn

Brown and drain sausage. Combine sausage and remaining ingredients in a two-quart casserole dish. Bake uncovered at 350° for 45 minutes.

EASY BREAKFAST BAKE

½ pound pork sausage
1 teaspoon salt
2¼ cups water
¾ cup quick grits
2 tablespoons butter
2 tablespoons all-purpose flour

¼ teaspoon black pepper
1 cup milk
½ cup cheddar cheese, shredded
4 eggs

Cook and crumble sausage. Drain; set aside drippings. Bring salted water to a boil and stir in grits. Cover and reduce heat to low. Cook 5 minutes more, stirring occasionally. Melt butter and stir in flour, black pepper, and milk. Cook, stirring to thicken. Add cheese; stir until blended. Add sausage and half of cheese sauce to grits. Pour into greased casserole dish. Make 4 indentions into grits mixture with the back of a large spoon. Break one egg into each indention. Bake at 325° for 13–18 minutes, depending on preferred doneness of eggs. Serve with remaining heated sauce.

COUNTRY BREAKFAST CASSEROLE

½ pound spicy or mild bulk
  pork sausage
½ cup finely chopped onion
4 cups frozen diced hash
  brown potatoes, thawed
  (about half a 32-ounce
  package)

1½ cups Colby/Monterey
  Jack cheese, shredded
  (6 ounces)
3 eggs, beaten
1 cup milk
¼ teaspoon pepper
Salsa

In a large skillet, thoroughly brown sausage and onion. Drain. In an 8x8x2-inch baking dish, layer potatoes, half of the cheese, sausage mixture, and remaining cheese. Combine eggs, milk, and pepper; pour over cheese. (May be covered and chilled overnight if necessary.) Bake, covered, at 350° for 50–55 minutes or until a knife inserted near center comes out clean. Transfer to a wire rack. Let stand for 10 minutes. Cut into squares and serve with salsa.

EGG CASSEROLE
Prepare the night before.

6 slices bread, cubed
1 pound bulk sausage, browned,
  drained, and crumbled
8 ounces sharp cheddar cheese,
  shredded

8–12 large eggs, beaten
1 teaspoon dry mustard
2 cups half-and-half

Grease a 13x9x2-inch baking dish with butter. Layer bread, sausage, and cheese in the dish. Mix beaten eggs with mustard and half-and-half. Pour egg mixture over layers in dish. Refrigerate uncovered casserole overnight. Bake, uncovered, at 350° for 30–35 minutes. If desired, add fried bacon strips to the top of casserole 5 minutes before baking time is complete.

EASY BREAKFAST STRATA

1 pound roll sausage
8 eggs
10 slices bread, cubed
3 cups milk
2 cups cheddar cheese, shredded
2 cups fresh mushrooms,
  sliced

1 10-ounce package frozen
  cut asparagus
2 tablespoons butter, melted
2 tablespoons flour
1 tablespoon dry mustard
2 teaspoons basil
1 teaspoon salt

In a large skillet, brown sausage; drain. In a large bowl, beat eggs. Add sausage, bread, milk, cheese, mushrooms, asparagus, butter, flour, mustard, basil, and salt. Mix thoroughly. Spoon into a greased 13x9x2-inch baking pan. Cover and refrigerate overnight. Bake at 350° for 60–70 minutes or until fork inserted at the center comes out clean. Refrigerate leftovers.

BLUEBERRY AND CREAM CHEESE STRATA

7 cups white bread cubes,
  no crusts (16-ounce loaf)
2 cups frozen or fresh
  blueberries (do not thaw
  frozen berries)
1 3-ounce package cream
  cheese, cut into ¼-inch cubes

4 eggs
2 cups milk
⅓ cup sugar
1 teaspoon vanilla extract
¼ teaspoon salt
¼ teaspoon ground nutmeg

Butter an 8-inch square baking dish. Put half of the bread cubes into baking dish and top with half of the blueberries and all of the cream cheese cubes. Top with remaining bread cubes and blueberries. In a mixing bowl, beat eggs, milk, sugar, vanilla, salt, and nutmeg. Beat well. Pour over bread mixture and refrigerate at least 20 minutes. May be refrigerated overnight if necessary. Bake uncovered at 325° for 1 hour.

SIMPLE SAUSAGE STRATA

6 slices bread, no crusts
1 pound bulk pork sausage, browned and drained
1 teaspoon prepared mustard
¾ cup Swiss cheese, shredded
3 eggs
1¼ cups milk
⅔ cup half-and-half
Pinch pepper

Grease a 13x9x2-inch baking dish. Place bread in baking dish and set aside. Stir mustard into cooked sausage. Sprinkle sausage mixture and cheese evenly over bread slices. In a mixing bowl, beat eggs, milk, half-and-half, and pepper. Pour egg mixture over cheese. Bake, uncovered, at 350° for 25–30 minutes or until fork inserted at the center comes out clean.

OVERNIGHT SAUSAGE SOUFFLÉ

1 pound link pork sausage, cut up
6 slices bread, cubed
1 cup medium cheddar cheese, shredded
4 eggs
2 cups milk
½ teaspoon salt
½ teaspoon dry mustard (optional)

Fry sausage and cut into pieces. Alternate layers of bread cubes, sausage, and cheese in a 2½-quart casserole dish. Beat eggs and add milk; then add salt and mustard. Pour egg mixture over the other ingredients. Cover and refrigerate overnight. Bake at 325° for 45–60 minutes.

SAUSAGE GRAVY
AND BISCUITS

GRAVY:

3 cups milk

6 tablespoons flour

Salt and pepper to taste

8 ounces spicy sausage

BISCUITS:

2¾ cups biscuit mix

¾ cup milk

Combine 3 cups milk, flour, salt, and pepper in a jar. Cover and shake until flour is dissolved. Pour into a skillet. Simmer for 15 minutes, stirring constantly to avoid scorching. Brown sausage in separate skillet, stirring until crumbly; drain. Add to gravy, stirring occasionally. Mix biscuit mix with ¾ cup milk in bowl until soft dough forms. Drop by spoonfuls onto ungreased baking sheet. Bake at 450° for 10 minutes or until golden brown. Spoon gravy over split biscuits.

MINI SAUSAGE PIZZAS

2 5-ounce jars sharp American cheese spread

¼ cup butter, softened

⅛ teaspoon cayenne pepper

1 pound bulk pork sausage, browned and well
    drained

12 English muffins, split

In a small mixing bowl, beat cheese, butter, and cayenne pepper. Add sausage and stir well. Spread on cut side of muffins. Place on a baking sheet and bake at 425° for 8–10 minutes or until golden brown.

WAFFLES WITH MAPLE SYRUP

4 eggs, separated
2 cups milk
3 cups sifted all-purpose
  flour

4 teaspoons baking powder
1 teaspoon salt
2 teaspoons sugar
2²/₃ cups butter, melted

Using an electric mixer, beat egg whites until fluffy; set aside. Beat egg yolks 1 minute. Add milk and beat another minute. Add sifted dry ingredients and beat 1 minute. Add melted butter and beat 15 seconds. Fold in stiffly beaten egg whites. Pour on hot waffle iron.

HOMEMADE MAPLE SYRUP:

2 cups sugar
¼ cup brown sugar
2 pounds white corn syrup

1 cup water
1 teaspoon vanilla extract
1 teaspoon maple flavoring

Mix sugars, corn syrup, and water together and bring just to boiling point (enough to melt sugars). Add vanilla and maple flavoring. Stir well and serve over waffles or pancakes. Keeps well in the refrigerator.

GINGERBREAD WAFFLES

¹/₄ cup sugar
2 tablespoons butter
2 tablespoons lard
1 egg, well beaten
¹/₂ cup molasses
¹/₂ teaspoon ginger

¹/₄ teaspoon cloves
1¹/₄ cups sifted flour
³/₄ teaspoon soda
¹/₂ teaspoon cinnamon
¹/₈ teaspoon salt
Hot water

In mixing bowl, cream together sugar, butter, and lard. Add beaten egg and molasses. Sift dry ingredients and add to butter mixture. Gradually add hot water. Beat hard to make a smooth batter. Cook in a preheated waffle iron.

SOUTHERN CORNMEAL WAFFLES

³/₄ cup yellow cornmeal
¹/₈ cup flour
¹/₄ teaspoon salt
¹/₄ teaspoon baking soda
¹/₂ teaspoon baking powder

1 teaspoon granulated sugar
1 egg, beaten
1 cup milk
2 teaspoons lemon juice
¹/₄ cup cooking oil

Sift together the first 6 ingredients. Stir in remaining ingredients. Cook on a greased waffle iron.

PUMPKIN PANCAKES

2 cups biscuit mix
2 tablespoons packed light
  brown sugar
2 teaspoons ground
  cinnamon
1 teaspoon ground allspice

1½ cups undiluted
  evaporated milk
½ cup solid packed pumpkin
2 tablespoons vegetable oil
2 eggs
1 teaspoon vanilla extract

Combine all dry ingredients. Add evaporated milk, pumpkin, oil, eggs, and vanilla. Beat until smooth. Pour ½ cup batter onto lightly greased, preheated griddle. Cook until bubbly on top and edges are dry. Turn; cook until golden brown. Serve warm pancakes with syrup.

NORWEGIAN PANCAKES

⅓ cup sour cream
⅓ cup small-curd cottage
  cheese
2 eggs, well beaten

¼ cup sifted flour
1 teaspoon granulated sugar
¼ teaspoon salt
1 can sliced peaches, warmed

Mix sour cream and cottage cheese. Blend well. Stir in next 4 ingredients. Pour batter onto hot, greased griddle. Brown pancakes on both sides. Top warm pancakes with warm peaches and serve immediately.

BERRY-STUFFED FRENCH TOAST

RASPBERRY SYRUP:

2 cups unsweetened
  raspberries
¾ cup packed brown sugar

3 tablespoons butter
1 teaspoon ground cinnamon
1½ teaspoons vanilla extract

FRENCH TOAST:

1 8-ounce package cream
  cheese, softened
½ cup sour cream
18 slices sourdough bread
1 teaspoon vanilla extract
½ cup raspberry preserves

6 eggs
¼ cup half-and-half
1½ teaspoons ground cinnamon
Confectioners' sugar and
  additional raspberries
  (optional)

NOTE: If you prefer a different fruit, simply substitute that fruit and the corresponding jam.

Mix raspberries, brown sugar, butter, and cinnamon in a saucepan. Bring mixture to a boil. Reduce heat and allow to simmer uncovered until syrup reaches desired consistency. Remove from heat and stir in vanilla. Set syrup aside. In a separate mixing bowl, beat the cream cheese and sour cream. Spread 3 tablespoons of cream cheese mixture on each slice of bread. Mix 1 teaspoon of vanilla with raspberry preserves. Spread over cream cheese mixture on 9 slices of bread. Top each slice with one of the remaining bread slices, being sure that the cream cheese side is covering the preserves. Mix eggs, half-and-half, and cinnamon in a shallow bowl. Dip both sides of bread in egg mixture. Cook each side on a hot griddle for 3–4 minutes or until golden brown. If desired, dust the toast with confectioners' sugar and use berries for garnish. Serve with raspberry syrup.

PRALINE SYRUP

2 cups dark corn syrup
1/3 cup dark brown sugar
1/2 cup water

1 cup pecan pieces
1/2 teaspoon vanilla extract

In a saucepan over medium heat, stir together syrup, sugar, and water. Bring to a boil; boil for 1 minute. Remove from heat; add pecans and vanilla. Pour syrup into hot jars, leaving 1/4-inch head space. Adjust caps. Process 10 minutes in a boiling water bath.

APPLE CIDER SYRUP

1/2 cup sugar
4 teaspoons cornstarch
1/2 teaspoon ground
   cinnamon

1 cup apple cider or
   apple juice
1 tablespoon lemon juice
2 tablespoons butter

In a saucepan, stir together sugar, cornstarch, and cinnamon. Add apple cider and lemon juice, stirring thoroughly. Cook mixture, stirring constantly, over medium heat until mixture is thickened and bubbly. Cook and stir 2 minutes more. Remove from heat. Stir in butter until it is melted. Serve over French toast, pancakes, or waffles.

HONEY-TOPPED
PECAN BREAKFAST BREAD

½ cup sugar
1–2 teaspoons ground cinnamon
¼ cup chopped pecans
2 8-ounce cans refrigerated crescent rolls
2 tablespoons butter, melted

HONEY TOPPING:

¼ cup sifted confectioners' sugar
2 tablespoons honey
2 tablespoons butter

1 teaspoon vanilla extract
¼ cup pecan halves

Mix sugar, cinnamon, and pecans. Set aside. Unroll crescent-roll dough and separate into 16 triangles. Brush each triangle with melted butter and sprinkle with sugar mixture. Roll up each triangle, starting from the shortest side opposite a point and rolling toward the point. Place 8 rolls, point side down, in a greased 9x5x3-inch loaf pan. Place remaining rolls on top of first layer. Bake at 325° for about 55 minutes or until done. Meanwhile, prepare the honey topping by combining all topping ingredients except pecans in a small saucepan. Heat until smooth and bubbly. Gradually stir in pecan halves. Cool for 15 minutes and drizzle over warm bread. Serve immediately.

CINNAMON-APPLE
BREAKFAST QUESADILLAS

2 6-inch flour tortillas
½ cup chunky applesauce, divided
1 tablespoon cinnamon-sugar, divided
¼ cup Monterey Jack cheese, shredded
2 tablespoons vanilla yogurt (optional)

Place one tortilla on an ungreased baking sheet. Spread ¼ cup applesauce over tortilla, reserving remainder for garnish. Sprinkle ½ tablespoon of cinnamon-sugar mixture over applesauce. Top with cheese and second tortilla. Sprinkle remaining cinnamon-sugar on top. Bake at 400° for 6–8 minutes or until golden brown. Allow to cool 2 minutes. Cut into quarters and serve with remaining applesauce and vanilla yogurt.

HOT FRUIT COMPOTE

1 can peaches, drained
1 can pears, drained
1 can pineapple chunks,
  drained
1 cup brown sugar
1 teaspoon cinnamon
¼ cup margarine
1 can cherry pie filling

Cut all fruit into bite-sized pieces. Add brown sugar, cinnamon, margarine, and pie filling. Stir all together. Cover and cook on low 3–6 hours.

WINTER SQUASH QUICHE

2 tablespoons chopped
    onion
2 teaspoons vegetable oil
2 cups Swiss cheese,
    shredded
1 1/2 cups milk

1 cup winter squash, cooked
    and mashed
3 eggs
1/4 teaspoon salt
1/8 teaspoon pepper
1/8 teaspoon ground nutmeg

Sauté onion in vegetable oil until tender. Remove to a greased 9-inch pie plate. Top with shredded cheese. In a mixing bowl, whisk milk, squash, eggs, salt, pepper, and nutmeg until smooth. Pour over Swiss cheese. Bake at 325° for 50–60 minutes or until fork inserted at center comes out clean.

CRUSTLESS CHEESE QUICHE

2 cups small-curd
    cottage cheese
2 cups Monterey Jack
    cheese, shredded
2 cups cheddar cheese,
    shredded
4 eggs, lightly beaten
2 tablespoons butter, melted

1 4-ounce can green chilies,
    chopped
2 tablespoons ripe olives,
    chopped
1/2 cup flour
1 teaspoon baking powder
1/2 teaspoon salt
Chopped tomatoes
Additional chopped ripe
    olives

Mix first 7 ingredients together. In a separate bowl, mix flour, baking powder, and salt. Add flour mixture to cheese mixture and mix well. Pour mixture into a greased 9-inch pie plate. Bake at 400° for 15 minutes. Reduce heat to 350° and bake 30 minutes longer or until fork inserted at center comes out clean. Use tomatoes and extra olives as a garnish.

FLORENTINE CREPE CUPS

⅔ cup flour   3 eggs
½ teaspoon salt   1 cup milk

FILLING:
1½ cups cheddar cheese, shredded
3 tablespoons flour
1 10-ounce package frozen chopped spinach,
    thawed and squeezed dry
1 4-ounce can mushrooms, drained
⅔ cup mayonnaise
3 eggs, lightly beaten
6 bacon strips, fried and crumbled
½ teaspoon salt
Pepper to taste

In a mixing bowl, whisk the flour, salt, eggs, and milk until smooth. Lightly grease an 8-inch nonstick skillet. Heat skillet and add 3 tablespoons of batter. Lift and tilt skillet to be sure bottom is evenly coated. Cook for a couple of minutes or until top appears dry. Remove to a greased muffin cup. Repeat with remaining batter. In a separate bowl, combine all filling ingredients. Pour ½ cup of filling into each crepe cup. Bake, uncovered, at 350°, until eggs are completely set (about 30 minutes).

HAM AND CHEESE CREPES

²/₃ cup cold water
²/₃ cup plus 4–6 tablespoons
  cold milk, divided
1 cup flour
2 eggs
¹/₄ teaspoon salt

¹/₄ cup butter, melted
2–4 tablespoons Dijon
  mustard
16 thin slices deli ham
2 cups cheddar cheese,
  shredded

Combine water, ²/₃ cup milk, flour, eggs, salt, and butter in a blender. Cover and blend until smooth. Refrigerate 30 minutes. Stir mixture and add remaining milk if batter is too thick. Lightly grease an 8-inch skillet. Heat skillet and add 3 tablespoons of batter. Lift and tilt to be sure bottom is evenly coated. Cook for a couple of minutes or until top appears dry. Turn and cook 15–20 seconds longer. Repeat with remaining batter. Grease skillet as needed. Stack crepes between layers of waxed paper and allow to cool. When cool, spread each crepe with mustard. Add a slice of ham and sprinkle with cheese. Roll crepes tightly. Place in two greased 11x7x2-inch baking dishes. Bake, uncovered, at 375° for 10–14 minutes or until thoroughly heated.

BUTTERMILK SCONES

4 cups flour
2–4 tablespoons sugar
1¹/₂ tablespoons
  baking powder

1 teaspoon salt
1 teaspoon baking soda
1 teaspoon butter, chilled
1¹/₂ cups buttermilk

Combine flour, sugar, baking powder, salt, and soda. Cut in butter until mixture resembles coarse crumbs. Make well in center of ingredients. Pour buttermilk into well, then stir until moistened. Turn dough onto a floured board. Knead gently 10–12 times. Form into a ball and flatten into a round. Using a pizza cutter, cut into 8 wedges. Place on ungreased baking sheet. Bake at 400° for 15–20 minutes or until done. Serve warm.

SWISS EGGS

3 tablespoons butter, divided
8 eggs
½ cup milk
½ teaspoon salt
⅛ teaspoon pepper
Seasoned salt
1 cup Swiss cheese, shredded
1 tablespoon dry
 bread crumbs

In a heavy skillet, melt 2 tablespoons butter. In a mixing bowl, beat together eggs, milk, salt, and pepper. Pour into skillet and cook, stirring constantly until eggs are set but still soft. Pour into a medium-sized, buttered baking dish. Sprinkle mixture with seasoned salt and cover with Swiss cheese. Dot with remaining butter. Sprinkle bread crumbs over top and bake at 400° for 10 minutes or until eggs are puffy and golden brown.

EGGS BRAVO

⅓ cup flour
⅛ teaspoon salt
Dash pepper
1¾ cups milk
4 ounces processed cheese,
 cubed
1½ cups fully cooked ham, cubed
4 hard-boiled eggs, chopped
½ cup mayonnaise
¼ cup sliced green onions
¼ cup chopped pimientos
6–8 English muffins, split
 and toasted

In a saucepan, stir together first 4 ingredients until smooth. Bring to a boil. Boil and stir until thickened (about 2 minutes). Add cheese. Cook and stir until cheese is melted. Stir in all remaining ingredients except English muffins. Heat through. Serve eggs over toasted English muffins.

COOKIES
AND CANDIES

I am still convinced that a good, simple,
homemade cookie is preferable to all
the store-bought cookies one can find.

JAMES BEARD

CHRISTMAS COOKIES

2 cups sugar
1/2 teaspoon salt
1 cup shortening
1 ounce baking ammonia

1 tablespoon vanilla extract
2 cups condensed milk
4 cups flour, just enough
    to stiffen

Mix all ingredients together. Roll out about 1/2-inch thick. Cut with favorite cookie cutters. Bake at 350° for 10 minutes. Ice with a vanilla icing and sugar sprinkles.

NOTE: Baking ammonia can be purchased through a baking catalog such as King Arthur Flour's Baking Catalog.

CHRISTMAS EVE COOKIES

1 cup sugar
1/2 cup butter
1/2 cup shortening
1 egg, separated
2 cups flour

1/2 teaspoon salt
1 1/2 tablespoons ground
    cinnamon
1 1/2 cups chopped nuts

Grease and flour a 10x15-inch pan. Cream sugar, butter, and shortening. Add egg yolk and dry ingredients. Press into pan. Beat egg white until foamy and spread very thinly over batter. Press on nuts. Bake at 350° for about 30 minutes. Cut into squares and serve.

HOLLY COOKIES

$\frac{1}{3}$ cup butter
16 marshmallows
1 teaspoon green food
  coloring

1 teaspoon vanilla extract
$2\frac{1}{2}$ cups whole cornflakes
Red cinnamon candy

Melt butter and marshmallows in double boiler. Blend in food coloring and vanilla. Place cornflakes in large bowl; pour mixture over cornflakes and mix lightly with fork. Drop cookies onto waxed paper or form into wreath. Sprinkle with cinnamon candy and allow to set.

SNOWMEN COOKIES

White chocolate almond bark
Nutter Butter sandwich cookies
Mini chocolate chips

Melt almond bark and spread the chocolate on the cookies. Place 2 mini chocolate chips side-by-side to make eyes.

SOUR CREAM CHRISTMAS COOKIES

1 cup Crisco
1 cup margarine
2 cups sugar
2 eggs
2 teaspoons baking soda
¾ teaspoon salt
1 teaspoon baking powder

2 teaspoons vanilla extract
1 teaspoon lemon juice
1 teaspoon nutmeg
6 cups flour
1 cup sour cream
1 cup buttermilk

Melt Crisco and margarine together. Cream with sugar, eggs, baking soda, salt, and baking powder; mix well. Add vanilla, lemon juice, and nutmeg. Alternately add flour, sour cream, and buttermilk. Chill overnight, uncovered. Roll and cut on floured surface. Bake at 375° for 5–8 minutes or until soft in middle.

ANISE CUTOUTS

½ cup shortening
1 cup sugar
2 eggs
1 teaspoon vanilla extract

2 cups flour
2 teaspoons baking powder
½ teaspoon salt
1 tablespoon aniseed

In a mixing bowl, cream together shortening and sugar. Add eggs and vanilla and mix thoroughly. In a separate bowl, mix flour, baking powder, and salt. Add to shortening mixture. Stir in aniseed. Refrigerate for 2 hours or until dough is easily handled. On a lightly floured board, roll dough to ⅛-inch thickness. Cut with cookie cutters. Place 1 inch apart on ungreased baking sheets. Bake at 325° for 7–10 minutes. Cool on wire racks.

GINGERBREAD MEN

2 cups sugar
1 cup shortening
2 eggs
½ cup molasses
4 cups flour
1 teaspoon ginger

1 teaspoon cloves
1 teaspoon nutmeg
1 teaspoon baking soda
¼ teaspoon salt
2 teaspoons cinnamon

Cream together sugar and shortening. Add eggs and molasses. Sift remaining ingredients and add to sugar mixture. Wrap tightly and place in refrigerator for several hours. Roll dough thin and cut with cookie cutter. Bake at 325° for 10–12 minutes. Use raisins, currants, mini chocolate chips, or mini M&Ms for eyes, nose, buttons, etc. Use colored icing for other details.

EASY GINGERBREAD CUTOUTS

1 18¼-ounce spice cake mix
¾ cup all-purpose flour
2 eggs
⅓ cup vegetable oil
⅓ cup molasses

2 teaspoons ground ginger
¾ cup canned cream cheese
   frosting, warmed slightly
Red-hot candies or other
   small decorative candies

Combine cake mix, flour, eggs, oil, molasses, and ginger. Mix thoroughly. Refrigerate for 30 minutes or until dough is easily handled. On a floured board, roll dough to ⅛-inch thickness. Cut with 5-inch cookie cutters that have been dipped in flour. Place 3 inches apart on ungreased baking sheets. Bake at 375° for 7–10 minutes or until edges are firm and bottom is lightly browned. Cool on wire racks. Decorate with cream cheese frosting and candies, as desired.

GINGER-MOLASSES COOKIES

2¼ cups margarine, softened
1 cup minus 1 tablespoon
  molasses
3 cups sugar
3 eggs

7¾ cups flour
1 tablespoon ginger
2 tablespoons baking soda
1 tablespoon cinnamon
1½ teaspoons salt

Mix together margarine, molasses, sugar, and eggs. Sift together flour, ginger, baking soda, cinnamon, and salt; add to molasses mixture. Roll into 1-inch balls. If desired, roll balls in a cinnamon-sugar mixture. Place on ungreased cookie sheets. Bake at 350° for 8–10 minutes or until light brown. These cookies freeze well.

SOFT MOLASSES COOKIES

1 cup sugar
1 cup molasses
2 heaping teaspoons soda
1 teaspoon salt
1 cup flour

1 cup cold water
1 teaspoon ginger
½ teaspoon cinnamon
½ teaspoon cloves

Mix all ingredients together; add enough flour that you can handle and roll out the dough. Roll thick and cut with a cookie cutter. Bake at 400° for appropximately 10 minutes.

CUTOUT COOKIES

2 cups sugar
2½ cups butter
3 eggs
8 cups flour
1 teaspoon baking soda

½ teaspoon salt
3 teaspoons baking powder
3 tablespoons milk
(more if needed)
1 teaspoon vanilla extract

In a large mixing bowl, on medium speed, cream together sugar, butter, and eggs. In a separate bowl, mix together flour, soda, salt, and baking powder. Alternately mix dry ingredients and milk with sugar mixture. Mix in vanilla. Roll dough to ¼–½-inch thickness. Cut with cookie cutters. Bake at 325° for 12 minutes or until golden. Ice with favorite icing and sprinkle with sugar sprinkles. This makes many cookies, so you may wish to cut the recipe in half.

CUTOUT SUGAR COOKIES

1 pound butter, softened
3 cups sugar
4 eggs
2 cups cream or evaporated
   milk
10 cups flour

½ teaspoon salt
2 teaspoons baking soda
6 teaspoons baking powder
2 teaspoons vanilla extract
½ teaspoon almond extract

Cream together butter and sugar. Add eggs and mix well. Stir in cream. In a separate bowl, sift together all dry ingredients. Add to butter mixture; stir in vanilla and almond extract. Mix well. Chill 1 hour. Roll out on floured surface; cut with cookie cutters. Bake at 350° for 5–7 minutes or until light golden. When cooled, ice as desired.

HOLIDAY FRUIT DROPS

1 cup shortening
2 cups brown sugar, packed
2 eggs
½ cup sour milk or ⅔ cup
    buttermilk
3½ cups flour
1 teaspoon baking soda

1 teaspoon salt
1 cup chopped nuts
2 cups candied cherries,
    cut into small pieces,
    or 1 cup candied cherries
    and 1 cup dates

Mix shortening, sugar, and eggs well. Stir in milk. Blend dry ingredients and stir into shortening mixture. Add nuts, dates, and cherries. Chill 1 hour. Heat oven. Drop dough by spoonfuls onto greased baking sheet or make into balls. Bake at 400° for 8–10 minutes.

OATMEAL COOKIES

4 cups quick-cooking oatmeal
2 cups light brown sugar
1 cup butter or margarine, melted
2 eggs, beaten
1 teaspoon salt
1 teaspoon almond flavoring or ½ teaspoon vanilla
    extract
½ cup coconut
½ cup chopped nuts (optional)

Combine all ingredients and refrigerate overnight. Drop by rounded teaspoons onto greased cookie sheet. Bake at 350° for 10 minutes.

RAISIN-WALNUT-OATMEAL COOKIES

1 cup flour
1 teaspoon ground cinnamon
½ teaspoon baking powder
½ teaspoon baking soda
¼ teaspoon salt
½ cup butter at room temperature
½ cup granulated sugar
½ cup packed brown sugar
1 large egg
1 teaspoon vanilla extract
1¼ cups quick-cooking oats
½ cup raisins
¾ cup chopped walnuts

Mix flour, cinnamon, baking powder, baking soda, and salt. In a separate large mixing bowl, beat together butter, sugar, brown sugar, egg, and vanilla until creamy. Using low speed, gradually add butter mixture to flour mixture. Beat just until blended. Beat in oats, raisins, and walnuts. Roll heaping tablespoonfuls of dough into balls. Place 2 inches apart on ungreased cookie sheets. Bake at 375° for 10–12 minutes or until light golden brown. Allow to cool.

KOURABIEDES
(Greek Christmas Cookies)

1 pound unsalted butter
  or margarine
3 tablespoons confectioners'
  sugar

2 egg yolks
1 teaspoon vanilla extract
5 cups sifted flour
Confectioners' sugar for
  topping

Cream butter until light and fluffy. Beat in sugar. Add egg yolks and vanilla. Gradually work in sifted flour to make a soft dough. You will need to discard the spoon and use your hands after a certain point. With floured hands shape into small crescents or oval shapes about ½-inch thick. Place one inch apart on ungreased cookie sheet. Bake at 375° for about 20 minutes or until bottoms are very lightly browned. Place cookies on a plate and sift confectioners' sugar over tops and sides. Cool thoroughly before storing.

CREAM CHEESE LOGS

½ cup butter
4 ounces cream cheese,
  softened
1 teaspoon vanilla extract
1¾ cups flour

1 tablespoon sugar
Dash salt
1 cup finely chopped pecans
Confectioners' sugar

In a mixing bowl, cream together the butter and cream cheese. Beat in vanilla. In a separate bowl, combine flour, sugar, and salt. Gradually add to butter mixture. Stir in pecans to form a crumbly dough. Shape tablespoonfuls into 2-inch logs. Place 2 inches apart on ungreased cookie sheet. Bake at 375° for 12–14 minutes or until golden brown. Roll warm cookies in confectioners' sugar. Cool on wire racks.

CHEWY CHOCOLATE COOKIES

½ cup shortening
1 cup sugar
1 large egg
1 teaspoon vanilla extract
1¾ cups flour
½ teaspoon baking soda
¼ teaspoon salt

½ cup cocoa
½ cup milk
½ cup chopped pecans
24 large marshmallows,
    cut in half
Pecan halves

CHOCOLATE FROSTING:
2 cups sifted confectioners' sugar
¼ cup plus 1 tablespoon cocoa
3 tablespoons butter, softened
¼ cup milk

Beat shortening on medium speed. Gradually add sugar. Beat well. Add egg and vanilla and again beat well. In a separate bowl combine flour, soda, salt, and cocoa. Slowly add to shortening mixture alternately with milk. When alternating begin and end with flour mixture, being sure to mix well after each addition. Finally stir in chopped pecans. Drop dough by rounded teaspoonfuls onto lightly greased cookie sheets. Bake at 350° for 8 minutes. After cookies have baked for 8 minutes, remove from oven. Place a marshmallow half, cut side down, on top of each cookie. Bake 2 minutes more. Remove to wire racks. Allow to cool completely before spreading with chocolate frosting and topping with a pecan half. To prepare chocolate frosting, combine all frosting ingredients. Beat on medium speed until light and fluffy.

ORANGE DROP COOKIES

⅔ cup margarine
¾ cup sugar
1 egg
½ cup orange juice
2 tablespoons grated orange
    rind

2 cups flour
½ teaspoon baking powder
½ teaspoon soda
½ teaspoon salt

ORANGE BUTTER ICING:
2 cups sifted confectioners' sugar
2 tablespoons butter
1 tablespoon grated orange rind
About 2 tablespoons orange juice

Mix margarine, sugar, and egg. Stir in orange juice and rind. Blend dry ingredients and stir in orange juice mixture. Drop by rounded teaspoonfuls 2 inches apart on ungreased baking sheet. Bake at 400° for 8–10 minutes. Allow to cool before icing with Orange Butter Icing. To make icing, blend confectioners' sugar and butter. Stir in orange rind and orange juice until smooth.

CANDIED PECANS

¼ cup butter
½ cup brown sugar
1 teaspoon cinnamon

2 cups pecan halves
Salt (optional)

Use a heavy skillet or pan. Cook ingredients over medium-low heat, stirring constantly until nuts are coated and sugar is golden brown (about 5 minutes). Spread on aluminum foil; sprinkle lightly with salt, if desired. Allow to cool.

PEANUT BUTTER CUPS

4 cups peanut butter
1 pound butter, melted
3 pounds confectioners' sugar

24 ounces chocolate chips
¾ stick paraffin

Mix peanut butter, butter, and confectioners' sugar together; stir well. Melt chips and paraffin together. Make balls out of first mixture and dip them into the chocolate mixture. Place on waxed paper to dry. Wrap in waxed paper.

PEANUT BRITTLE

2 cups granulated sugar
½ cup light corn syrup
1 cup water

1 teaspoon butter
¼ teaspoon soda
2¼ cups salted peanuts

Butter a cookie sheet thoroughly. Spread salted peanuts over the bottom of cookie sheets. Set aside. In a saucepan, mix sugar, corn syrup, and water. Cook until medium brown in color, about 25 minutes. Be sure to stir often. Remove from heat. Stir in remaining ingredients. Pour over peanuts immediately. Allow to cool. Break into pieces.

ENGLISH TOFFEE

1 cup sugar
1 cup butter
1 teaspoon vanilla extract

6 ½-ounce Hershey bars
Chopped pecans

Cover a cookie sheet with aluminum foil and spray with nonstick cooking spray. Cook sugar and butter to hard crack, on medium heat, until they turn brown. Add vanilla. Pour ingredients into pan and spread out to ⅛–¼-inch thickness. Break up Hershey bars; lay on top of hot toffee. Spread. Sprinkle with nuts. Cool and break into pieces.

OHIO BUCKEYES

1 cup margarine, melted
2 cups peanut butter
4 cups confectioners' sugar
1 teaspoon vanilla extract

2x2-inch piece of paraffin
3 cups chocolate chips
  (not imitation chocolate)

Cream together all ingredients except paraffin and chocolate. Chill in refrigerator a few hours, then roll into balls approximately ¾-inch in diameter. Chill the balls in refrigerator at least 8 hours. Melt paraffin and chocolate in double boiler. Using a toothpick, dip each ball into the chocolate mixture, twirling off excess chocolate. Place on waxed paper to set up.

ROCKY ROAD CANDY

1 bag semi-sweet chocolate chips
½ bag colored miniature marshmallows
⅓ cup chopped pecans

Melt chocolate over low heat, or use a double boiler or microwave. Stir in marshmallows and pecans. Spoon onto waxed paper. Form into a log. Refrigerate 2 hours. Slice into ½-inch pieces.

CHOCOLATE DRIZZLED PEANUT BUTTER FUDGE

1½ cups sugar
1 cup (5 ounces) evaporated
  milk
¼ cup butter
1 7-ounce jar marshmallow crème

1 cup chunky peanut butter
1 teaspoon vanilla extract
2 squares (1 ounce each)
  semisweet chocolate

Grease an 8- or 9-inch square pan. Melt sugar, milk, and butter. (Microwave on high 6 minutes, stirring halfway through.) Cook 4–6 minutes more, or until small amount of sugar forms soft ball when dropped in water, or until it reaches 236°. Add the remaining ingredients, except the chocolate. Beat until well blended. Pour into pan. Cool 30 minutes. Melt chocolate 1–2 minutes. Stir after 30 seconds. Drizzle over top of fudge.

MOCHA FUDGE

1 cup chopped pecans
3 cups semisweet chocolate
  chips
1 14-ounce can sweetened
  condensed milk

2 tablespoons strong brewed
  coffee, room temperature
1 teaspoon ground cinnamon
⅛ teaspoon salt
1 teaspoon vanilla extract

Line an 8-inch square baking pan with aluminum foil. Butter the foil and set pan aside. Microwave pecans on high for 4 minutes, being sure to stir after each minute. In a 2-quart microwave safe bowl, mix chocolate chips, milk, coffee, cinnamon, and salt. Microwave on high for 1½ minutes. Stir until smooth. Add pecans and vanilla to chocolate mixture and stir thoroughly. Pour into pan. Cover and refrigerate until firm, about 2 hours. Remove from pan and cut into squares of desired size.

ORANGE MARBLE FUDGE

1½ teaspoons plus ¾ cup
butter, divided
3 cups sugar
¾ cup whipping cream
1 10–12-ounce package
vanilla or white chips

1 7-ounce jar marshmallow
crème
3 teaspoons orange extract
12 drops yellow food
coloring
5 drops red food coloring

Using the 1½ teaspoons of butter, generously grease a 13x9x2-inch pan. In a saucepan, mix the sugar, cream, and ¾ cup butter. Cook, stirring constantly, over low heat until sugar dissolves. Bring to a boil. Continue to cook and stir for 4 more minutes. Remove from heat. Add white chips and marshmallow crème. Set aside one cup of mixture. Add orange extract and food coloring to remaining mixture. Stir until completely blended. Pour into greased pan. Drop tablespoonfuls of remaining mixture over the top of orange mixture. Using a knife, cut white mixture through orange mixture to swirl. Cover and refrigerate until firm. Cut into desired size squares.

PEPPERMINT DIVINITY

2⅔ cups sugar
⅔ cup light corn syrup
½ cup water
2 egg whites

2 teaspoons peppermint
extract
Pink food coloring
⅔ cup broken nuts (optional)

Heat sugar, corn syrup, and water in 2-quart saucepan over low heat, stirring constantly until sugar is dissolved. Cook, while stirring, to 260° on candy thermometer or until small amount of mixture dropped into very cold water forms a hard ball. Remove from heat. Beat egg whites until stiff peaks form; continue beating while pouring hot syrup in a thin stream into egg whites. Add peppermint extract and food coloring. The mixture should hold its shape. Add nuts if desired. Drop by spoonfuls onto waxed paper.

QUICK CHOCOLATE TRUFFLES

2 10–12-ounce packages milk chocolate chips
1 8-ounce carton frozen whipped topping, thawed
1¼ cups graham cracker crumbs

Microwave chocolate chips on medium-high heat for 1 minute. Stir; microwave 10–20 seconds longer until chips are melted. Stir occasionally during melting process. Allow to cool for about 30 minutes; stir occasionally. Fold in whipped topping. Drop rounded teaspoonfuls onto waxed paper-lined cookie sheets. Freeze until firm, about 1½ hours. Shape into balls and roll in crushed graham crackers. Refrigerate in airtight containers. If desired, you may freeze truffles and remove from freezer 30 minutes before serving.

OLD-FASHIONED TAFFY
Requires two people to make

1 cup sugar
1 cup dark corn syrup
2 tablespoons water
1 tablespoon apple cider vinegar
1 piece of butter, the size of a peanut
½ teaspoon baking soda

Place first 5 ingredients in a pan; bring to a boil. Boil until mixture forms a hard ball in a cup of cold water. Add baking soda and stir well. Pour into buttered pan. When cool, pull until shiny and ready to cut.

DESSERTS

My meditation of him shall be sweet:
I will be glad in the Lord.

PSALM 104:34

CHEESECAKE

1 3-ounce package any
  flavor Jell-O
1 cup boiling water
1 12-ounce can evaporated
  skim milk (refrigerated for
  24 hours)

1 8-ounce package cream
  cheese, softened to room
  temperature
1 cup sugar

CRUST:

3 cups graham crackers,
  crushed
½ cup sugar

1 teaspoon cinnamon
  (optional)
1 cup margarine, melted

Mix Jell-O and water. Set aside to cool. Prepare graham cracker crust by mixing crust ingredients together; press into a greased 13x9x2-inch pan. Whip milk until peaks form. Mix cream cheese and sugar; add to whipped milk. Mix Jell-O with cream cheese mixture. Pour mixture over crust. Refrigerate until set.

LOW-FAT MINI CHEESECAKES

12 vanilla wafers
2 8-ounce packages nonfat
  cream cheese, softened
2 tablespoons flour

½ cup sugar
1 teaspoon vanilla extract
½ cup egg substitute
½ can light pie filling

Line muffin tins with foil cupcake papers. Place one vanilla wafer in bottom of each paper. Blend cream cheese until smooth. Add all remaining ingredients except pie filling. Mix well. Pour enough of the cream cheese mixture over each vanilla wafer to make cups ¾ full. Bake at 325° for 30 minutes. Cool slightly and remove from muffin tins. Chill completely. Before serving, top each cheesecake with pie filling.

FROZEN PEPPERMINT CHEESECAKE

1 8-ounce package cream cheese, softened

1 14-ounce can condensed milk

1 cup crushed hard peppermint candy

2 cups whipping cream, whipped

1 9-inch pre-made chocolate piecrust

In large mixing bowl, beat cream cheese until fluffy. Gradually beat in condensed milk. Stir in crushed candy. Fold in whipping cream. Pour into crust. Garnish as desired. Freeze 6 hours or until firm. Return leftovers to freezer.

Ideas for garnishes: crushed peppermint candies or milk chocolate shavings

CRANBERRY SAUCE CAKE

1½ cups whole cranberry sauce

1 cup mayonnaise

Grated rind of 1 orange

⅓ cup orange juice

1 cup chopped nuts

3 cups sifted flour

1½ cups sugar

1 teaspoon baking soda

1 teaspoon salt

FROSTING:

2 tablespoons margarine

2 cups confectioners' sugar

¼ cup whole cranberry sauce

Mix together cake ingredients. Pour into tube or Bundt pan. Bake at 350° until cake is done, about 1 hour and 15 minutes. Cool and frost. To make frosting, cream together margarine and confectioners' sugar; add cranberry sauce. Beat until very creamy.

APPLE DANISH CHEESECAKE

1 cup flour
½ cup ground almonds
¼ cup sugar

½ cup cold butter
¼ teaspoon almond extract

FILLING:

1 8-ounce package cream
 cheese, softened
¼ cup sugar

¼ teaspoon cream of tartar
1 egg

TOPPING:

⅓ cup packed brown sugar
1 tablespoon flour
1 teaspoon ground cinnamon

4 cups thinly sliced tart apple,
 peeled
⅓ cup slivered almonds

Mix flour, almonds, and sugar in a small bowl. Cut in butter to form a crumbly mixture. Add almond extract. Form dough into a ball and place it between two pieces of waxed paper. Roll dough into a 10-inch circle and place it in a greased 9-inch spring form pan. Carefully press dough into bottom of pan and up the sides. Chill for 30 minutes. Meanwhile, beat together cream cheese, sugar, and cream of tartar until smooth. Add egg. Beat on low until just combined. Pour over crust. In another bowl, combine first three topping ingredients. Add apples, stirring until coated. Spoon over the filling. Top with slivered almonds. Bake at 350° for 40–45 minutes or until light brown. Cool for 10 minutes. Loosen edges with a knife and cool 1 hour longer. Refrigerate overnight, then remove sides from pan.

PUMPKIN CRANBERRY CHEESECAKE

CRUST:

1½ cups vanilla wafers,
crushed (33 wafers)
¼ cup sugar

¼ cup ground pecans
¼ cup butter, melted

FILLING:

1 8-ounce package cream
cheese, softened
1 cup canned pumpkin
½ cup sugar
¼ cup brown sugar, packed
2 teaspoons lemon juice

1 teaspoon ground cinnamon
1 teaspoon vanilla extract
½ teaspoon ground nutmeg
1 8-ounce carton Cool
Whip, thawed

CRANBERRY SAUCE:

1½ cups whole cranberries
½ cup water

½ cup sugar
2 teaspoons cornstarch

Toss vanilla wafer crumbs, ¼ cup sugar, pecans, and melted butter in a large mixing bowl. Press mixture into bottom and 2 inches up sides of an 8-inch spring form pan. Bake at 350° for 5 minutes. Cool on wire rack. In a large mixing bowl, beat cream cheese, pumpkin, ½ cup sugar, brown sugar, lemon juice, cinnamon, vanilla, and nutmeg. Fold in Cool Whip. Turn mixture into cooled crust and chill for at least 4 hours. Combine cranberries, water, ½ cup sugar, and cornstarch in a saucepan. Cook until mixture boils, stirring constantly. Cook and stir 2 minutes longer. Cool to room temperature, then chill. Spoon over cheesecake. Garnish servings with additional Cool Whip, if desired.

EASY-TO-PLEASE FRUITCAKE

1 pound pitted dates, cut in small pieces and
    softened
8 ounces candied pineapple, chopped
8 ounces candied cherries, chopped
3 cups pecans, chopped
1 cup sifted flour
1 cup sugar
1 teaspoon baking powder
1/4 teaspoon salt
4 eggs, well beaten
1 teaspoon vanilla extract

Mix all ingredients well. Place in paper-lined angel food cake pan. Bake at 325° approximately 1½ hours or until done.

FESTIVE FRUITCAKE

2 eggs
2 cups water
1/4 cup oil
2 packages date bread mix
2 cups pecans, finely
    chopped

2 cups raisins
2 cups red and green
    candied cherries
1 cup banana
1 can fruit cocktail, drained

Combine eggs, water, and oil. Combine date bread mix, pecans, raisins, cherries, banana, and fruit cocktail; add to egg mixture. Bake at 350° in greased and floured Bundt pan for 75–85 minutes, until tests done. Cool in pan 30 minutes; loosen edges and remove from pan. Cool completely. Wrap in plastic wrap or foil. Refrigerate 2 weeks or freeze for up to 3 months. Glaze with warm corn syrup before serving. Decorate with frosting, candied cherries, and nuts.

HOLLYDAY CAKE

2 cups flour, sifted
2 teaspoons baking soda
½ teaspoon salt
½ teaspoon cinnamon
¼ teaspoon cloves
1 cup seedless raisins

1 cup mixed candied fruit
½ cup butter or margarine
1 cup sugar
1 egg
1 teaspoon vanilla extract
1½ cups applesauce
½ cups nuts (optional)

Sift together flour, baking soda, salt, and spices. Combine ½ cup of this mixture with fruits. Cream butter and sugar. Stir in egg, vanilla, and applesauce. Add dry ingredients gradually; mix well. Stir in fruit and nuts. Pour into a greased cake pan or loaf pan. Bake in a slow oven at 325° for 1½ hours. Cool and decorate.

FRUIT COCKTAIL CAKE

1 cup flour
1 teaspoon baking soda
1 cup sugar
¼ teaspoon salt

1 can fruit cocktail
1 egg, slightly beaten
½ cup brown sugar
½ cup chopped nuts

Combine flour, baking soda, sugar, and salt in a mixing bowl. Stir in fruit cocktail. Add egg. Pour mixture into an 8-inch greased and floured cake pan. Sprinkle with brown sugar and nuts. Bake at 350° for 40–45 minutes.

MOTHER'S APPLE CAKE

2 cups sugar
¾ cup vegetable oil
1 teaspoon salt
1 teaspoon vanilla extract
2 large eggs
2½ cups flour

1 teaspoon baking soda,
    mixed into flour
3 cups diced apples
1 cup chopped nuts
1 teaspoon cinnamon
½ cup raisins (optional)
Whipped topping (optional)

SAUCE:

1 cup brown sugar
½ cup heavy cream

¼ cup butter
½ teaspoon cinnamon

Mix sugar and oil well. Add salt, vanilla, and eggs. Cream well. Add flour, baking soda, apples, nuts, cinnamon, and raisins. Spread into a 13x9x2-inch pan. Bake at 350° for 50–60 minutes. When cake is nearly done, mix all sauce ingredients in a saucepan. Bring to a boil and remove from heat. Pour sauce over hot cake. If desired, serve cake with whipped topping.

WHIPPED CREAM CAKE

1½ cups butter
3 cups sugar
6 eggs

3 cups flour
½ pint whipping cream

Cream butter and sugar. Add eggs, one at a time, beating after each addition. Beginning and ending with flour, alternately add flour and cream. (Do not whip cream.) Lightly grease and flour a tube pan. Pour mixture into pan and bake at 300° for 2 hours.

PEPPERMINT STICK CAKE

2²/₃ cups flour
3 teaspoons baking powder
1 teaspoon salt
¹/₂ cup shortening
1¹/₂ cups sugar
1¹/₄ cups milk
1 egg yolk

1 teaspoon vanilla extract
3 egg whites
¹/₂ cup peppermint stick
  candy, finely ground
¹/₂ cup peppermint stick
  candy, coarsely ground
White icing

Sift flour and measure. Sift again with baking powder and salt. Cream shortening. Continue creaming while gradually adding 1¹/₂ cups sugar and 3 tablespoons milk. Add egg yolk and vanilla to remaining milk. Add sifted dry ingredients alternately with milk to creamed mixture. Beat egg whites until stiff but not dry. Beat in remaining sugar. Fold in cake batter. Pour into two 9-inch pans or one 13x9-inch pan and sprinkle with finely ground candy. Bake at 375° for 25 minutes. Cool. Ice with white icing and sprinkle with coarsely ground candy.

BLACK MAGIC CAKE

1¹/₄ cups flour
2 cups sugar
¹/₄ cup cocoa
2 teaspoons baking soda
1 teaspoon baking powder
1 teaspoon salt
2 eggs
¹/₂ cup oil

1 teaspoon vanilla extract
1 cup sour milk
  (2 tablespoons vinegar
  in 1 cup milk)
1 cup strong coffee
  (2 teaspoons coffee in
  1 cup boiling water)

Combine all dry ingredients. Add the liquid ingredients. The mixture will be thin. Bake in a 13x9x2-inch baking dish at 350° for 30 minutes.

CHOCOLATE-MINT BARS

1 cup butter
4 squares unsweetened
　chocolate
2 cups sugar
1 cup all-purpose flour
1 teaspoon vanilla extract
$\frac{1}{2}$ teaspoon salt

4 eggs
1 cup walnuts, coarsely
　chopped
$\frac{3}{4}$ cup confectioners' sugar
1 tablespoon water
$\frac{1}{4}$ teaspoon peppermint extract
Green food coloring

In small saucepan, over very low heat, melt butter and chocolate, stirring often. Pour melted mixture into large mixing bowl and add sugar, flour, vanilla, salt, and eggs. With mixer at low speed, beat ingredients until blended, occasionally scraping bowl with rubber spatula. Stir in nuts. Pour chocolate mixture into greased 13x9x2-inch pan. Bake at 350° for 35 minutes or until toothpick inserted at center comes out clean. Cool in pan. In a smaller mixing bowl, use a spoon to mix confectioners' sugar, water, and peppermint extract until icing is smooth. Stir in enough green food coloring to tint a pretty green color. Drizzle over cooled chocolate bars in pan. When icing hardens, cut into 32 bars. Cover and refrigerate to use up within 1 week.

FUDGE-TOPPED BROWNIES

1 cup butter, melted
2 cups sugar
1 cup unsifted flour
⅔ cup cocoa
½ teaspoon baking powder
2 eggs
½ cup milk

3 teaspoons vanilla extract
1 cup chopped nuts (optional)
1 12-ounce package semi-
    sweet chocolate chips
1 14-ounce can
    condensed milk

In a large mixing bowl, combine butter, sugar, flour, cocoa, baking powder, eggs, milk, and 1½ teaspoons vanilla. Beat thoroughly. Stir in nuts. Grease a 13x9x2-inch pan and evenly spread mixture in pan. Bake at 350° for 40 minutes or until brownies just begin to pull away from sides of pan. When brownies are nearly done, begin to mix icing. Using a heavy saucepan, over low heat, melt chocolate chips, condensed milk, and remaining portion of vanilla. Remove from heat. Immediately spread over hot brownies. Cool, chill, and cut into bars.

PUMPKIN PIE
DESSERT SQUARES

1 box yellow cake mix, divided   ½ cup butter or margarine,
1 egg   melted

FILLING:

3 cups (1 pound 14-ounce   2 eggs
   can) pumpkin pie mix   ⅔ cup milk

TOPPING:

1 cup reserved cake mix   ¼ cup butter, softened to
¼ cup sugar   room temperature
1 tablespoon cinnamon

Grease bottom only of 13x9x2-inch pan. Reserve 1 cup of the cake mix for topping. Combine remaining cake mix, egg, and melted butter. Press into bottom of pan. Mix filling ingredients until smooth and pour over bottom layer. Mix topping ingredients and sprinkle over the top of filling. Bake at 350° for 40–45 minutes or until knife inserted in the middle comes out clean. If desired, serve with whipped topping. For more of a cinnamon flavor, you may increase the amount of sugar and cinnamon in the topping.

SOUTHERN PECAN PIE

SINGLE CRUST PLAIN PASTRY:

1 cup all-purpose flour	6 tablespoons shortening
½ teaspoon salt	2–3 tablespoons very cold water

FILLING:

1 cup brown sugar, firmly packed	2 tablespoons butter, melted
1 cup light corn syrup	⅛ teaspoon salt
4 eggs	1 cup pecan halves

Prepare single crust pastry by spooning flour into dry measuring cup. Pour flour into mixing bowl and add salt. Stir to blend. Cut in half of shortening until mixture resembles coarse cornmeal. Cut in remaining shortening until crumbles are pea-sized. Add water, a little at a time, with fork. Shape dough into firm ball. Roll out on lightly floured surface. Place loosely in a 9-inch pie dish. Dough should be 1 inch wider than dish. Fold edge under. Moisten rim of pan. Flute edges of pastry. Prepare filling by combining all ingredients except pecans. Beat with rotary beater until smooth. Pour into unbaked pastry. Sprinkle with pecan halves. Bake at 375° for 40–45 minutes.

CHOCOLATE PEANUT BUTTER PIE

2 cups peanut butter, extra crunchy	1 cup skim milk
1 8-ounce package fat free cream cheese, softened	3 8-ounce containers whipped topping
2 cups confectioners' sugar	3 chocolate piecrusts

Mix peanut butter and cream cheese until smooth. Add confectioners' sugar, milk, and 12 ounces (1½ containers) of whipped topping. Blend thoroughly and pour into piecrusts, spreading evenly. Top each pie with 4 ounces whipped topping. These pies freeze and keep well. For added freshness, store pies in 1-gallon freezer bags.

BLACK FOREST CREAM PIE

1 15-ounce package all ready piecrusts

FILLING:
6 ounces semi-sweet baking chocolate, chopped
2 tablespoons margarine
¼ cup confectioners' sugar
1 8-ounce package cream cheese, softened
1 21-ounce can cherry fruit pie filling

TOPPING:
1 cup whipping cream, whipped
1 ounce semi-sweet baking chocolate, grated

Using a 9-inch pie pan with a removable bottom, prepare one crust according to package directions. Bake at 450° until lightly browned, 9–11 minutes. Allow to cool completely. Leftover crust may be refrigerated for a later use. While crust is cooling, melt chocolate and margarine over low heat, being sure to stir continually. When melted, remove from heat. In a bowl, beat together confectioners' sugar and cream cheese until smooth. Stir in chocolate mixture; beat until smooth. Fold in 1 cup of pie filling. Spread mixture evenly in prepared pie shell. Chill 1 hour. In a separate bowl, combine whipping cream and grated chocolate. Spread evenly over cooled chocolate layer. Spread any remaining pie filling around outer edge of pie. Refrigerate until ready to serve. If desired, garnish with chocolate curls.

APPLE CRANBERRY PIE

¹/₄ cup sugar
³/₄ cup brown sugar
¹/₃ cup all-purpose flour
1 teaspoon cinnamon
4 cups pared, sliced, tart apples

2 cups fresh or frozen
   cranberries
Pastry for double crust,
   9-inch pie
2 tablespoons butter

In a large mixing bowl, combine sugar, brown sugar, flour, and cinnamon. Add apples and cranberries. Mix well. Turn mixture into pastry-lined pie dish. Dot with butter. Cover with second half of crust. Cut slits in top crust. Seal edges. Bake at 425° for 40 minutes or until golden brown.

VERY BERRY PIE

Pastry for a double crust,
   9-inch pie
1 cup sugar
¹/₃ cup flour

5 cups mixed berries
   (blueberries, raspberries,
   and sliced strawberries)
1 tablespoon lemon juice
1 tablespoon butter

Prepare desired pastry and divide in half. Roll out one portion to fit a 9-inch pie plate. Place in plate and trim edges evenly. In a bowl, combine sugar and flour. Add berries and lemon juice. Toss berries to completely coat. Transfer berry mixture to pastry-lined pie plate. Dot berry mixture with butter. Roll remaining pastry into a 12-inch circle. Place on top of pie filling. Cut slits to vent. Trim dough to ¹/₂ inch beyond pie plate. Fold top of pastry under bottom pastry. Seal and flute edges. Place pie on baking sheet. Bake at 375° for 50 minutes or until pie is done.

*If you choose to use frozen berries, toss them with sugar mixture while frozen. Allow to sit 15–30 minutes or until partially thawed before transferring them to crust-lined plate.

MOM'S GINGERBREAD

½ cup butter
1 cup sugar
1 cup molasses
⅔ cup milk
2 eggs

½ teaspoon salt
3 cups flour
2 teaspoons baking soda
2 teaspoons cinnamon
2 teaspoons ginger

EASY LEMON SAUCE:

1 package lemon pudding
   and pie filling
½ cup sugar

3 cups water
1 egg

For gingerbread, mix all ingredients together. Pour into loaf pan. Bake at 325° until it springs back when lightly touched. Serve plain or topped with lemon sauce or whipped topping. To make Easy Lemon Sauce, combine pudding mix, sugar, and ¼ cup water in saucepan. Add egg; blend well. Add remaining water. Cook and stir over medium heat until it comes to full boil. Serve over warm gingerbread.

CRANBERRY NUT LOAF

1 8-ounce package
   cream cheese
⅓ cup margarine
1¼ cups sugar
1 teaspoon vanilla extract
3 eggs
2 tablespoons lemon juice

1 teaspoon lemon peel
2¼ cups flour
2 teaspoons baking powder
½ teaspoon baking soda
1½ cups chopped cranberries
1 cup chopped walnuts or
   pecans

In mixing bowl, beat cream cheese, margarine, sugar, and vanilla until well blended; add eggs one at a time. Mix in lemon juice and lemon peel, then flour, baking powder, and baking soda. Add cranberries and nuts. Bake at 325° for 1 hour and 15 minutes.

PUMPKIN ICE CREAM ROLL

¾ cup flour
2 teaspoons pumpkin
    pie spice
1 teaspoon baking powder
Dash salt
3 eggs
1 cup sugar

⅔ cup pumpkin
Confectioners' sugar
1 quart butter pecan ice
    cream, softened
Whipped cream (optional)
Toasted, chopped pecans
    (optional)

In a small bowl, combine first four ingredients. In a separate mixing bowl, beat eggs on high until they are pale yellow. Slowly add sugar. Stir in pumpkin and then slowly add dry mixture. Line a 15x10x1-inch pan with waxed paper. Grease and flour the paper. Pour batter into pan and bake at 375° for 15 minutes. When finished baking, turn cake out onto a linen towel that has been sprinkled with confectioners' sugar. Remove waxed paper and roll cake up in towel. Allow to cool. When completely cool, unroll cake. Place on baking sheet without the towel. Spread ice cream to within 1 inch of sides. Roll cake again. Cover and freeze. Allow to thaw for a few minutes before slicing. If desired, top cake with a sprinkling of confectioners' sugar, whipped topping, and toasted pecans.

CUSTARD
RAISIN BREAD PUDDING

4–5 slices raisin bread
2 cups milk, scalded
1 tablespoon butter
1/4 teaspoon salt

1/2 cup sugar
2 eggs, lightly beaten
1 teaspoon vanilla extract
Ground cinnamon

Soak bread in scalded milk for five minutes. Add butter, salt, sugar, eggs, and vanilla. Mix well. Pour into greased 1-quart casserole dish. Sprinkle lightly with cinnamon. Place casserole in pan of hot water in middle of oven. Bake for 45–50 minutes or until center is firm.

BANANA PUDDING PIE

2 bananas, sliced
1 Oreo piecrust
1 3 1/8-ounce box French vanilla instant pudding
1 8-ounce container frozen whipped topping,
   thawed
Crushed Oreos (optional)

Place sliced bananas in bottom of piecrust. Prepare pudding according to package directions. Pour pudding over bananas. Allow to set. When pudding is set, top with whipped topping. Garnish with crushed Oreos, if desired. Refrigerate until ready to serve.

MAIN DISHES

One of the pleasantest of all emotions
is to know that I,
with my brain and my hands,
have nourished my beloved few,
that I have concocted a stew or a story,
a rarity or a plain dish,
to sustain them truly against
the hungers of the world.

M.F.K. FISHER

ROAST BEEF AND POTATOES

1 beef roast, any cut
2 garlic cloves, thinly sliced
1 teaspoon dried thyme
1½ teaspoons pepper, divided

3 tablespoons olive oil
7 small red potatoes,
    cut into chunks
½ cup beef broth

Cut small slits in beef. Stuff each slit with one garlic slice. Mix thyme and 1 teaspoon of the pepper. Rub thyme mixture over beef. Place oil in Dutch oven and brown beef on all sides. Toss remaining pepper with potatoes. Add to the Dutch oven. Pour broth over meat and potatoes. Cover and bake at 300° for 4 hours or until tender.

EXCELLENT POT ROAST

1 6-pound rolled boneless
    chuck roast
2 tablespoons vegetable oil
1 large onion, chopped
2 medium carrots, chopped

1 celery rib, chopped
2 cups water
1 14½-ounce can beef broth
2 bay leaves

GRAVY:

¼ cup butter
¼ cup flour

1 teaspoon lemon juice
4 drops hot pepper sauce

In a Dutch oven, brown roast on all sides in oil. Drain any excess oil. Add vegetables to pan. In a separate saucepan, combine water, broth, and bay leaves. Bring to a boil and pour over contents of Dutch oven. Cover roast and bake at 320° for 4 hours or until meat is tender, turning once. Transfer roast and vegetables to serving platter and keep warm. Discard the bay leaves. In a saucepan over medium heat, melt butter. Slowly stir in flour until smooth. Stir in pan juices and bring to a boil. Cook and stir for 2 minutes. Stir in lemon juice and hot pepper sauce. Serve gravy with roast and vegetables.

DELUXE ROAST BEEF

3 or more pounds roast beef
1–2 onions
1 can cream of celery soup

1 can cream of mushroom
  soup
1/2 soup can water

Line a 13x9-inch baking dish with foil, making sure there is enough foil to cover and seal the meat. Cut off as much fat from meat as possible. Place meat in center of foil-lined pan. Slice onion. Place onion on top and at sides of meat. In a medium-sized bowl, combine the soups. Add water. Stir mixture well. Spoon over the beef, moistening all visible meat. Seal the meat in aluminum foil. Bake at 325° for about 45 minutes per pound or as long as possible without burning it. If you like, you may add thyme, sage, or other herbs and spices to the gravy. Serve with mashed potatoes and another vegetable.

SAVORY POT ROAST

2 tablespoons vegetable oil
3 1/2–4 pounds beef round
  or chuck pot roast
1 can cream of mushroom
  soup
1 package onion soup mix

1 1/4 cups water, divided
6 medium potatoes, quartered
6 carrots cut into 2-inch
  pieces
2 tablespoons all-purpose
  flour

In a 6-quart Dutch oven, heat oil and cook roast until all sides are browned. Spoon off fat. Stir in soups and 1 cup of water. Reduce heat to low. Cover and simmer for 2 hours or until meat is tender. Turn occasionally. Add potatoes and carrots. Cover and cook for 40 more minutes or until meat and vegetables are fork-tender. Remove meat and vegetables to serving platter. Cook sauce over medium heat until it is slightly thickened. In a cup, stir together flour and remaining water until smooth. Gradually stir flour mixture into Dutch oven. Cook until mixture boils and thickens, stirring occasionally. Serve gravy with roast.

BEEF STEW

2 tablespoons cooking oil
2 pounds beef stew meat (use venison if you prefer)
3 large onions, coarsely chopped
2 garlic cloves, crushed
1 tablespoon Worcestershire sauce
1 bay leaf
1 teaspoon dried oregano
1 tablespoon salt
1 teaspoon pepper
7 potatoes, peeled and quartered
1 pound carrots, peeled and cut into 1-inch pieces
¼ cup all-purpose flour
¼ cup cold water
Bottled browning sauce (optional)

Heat oil in a large Dutch oven. Brown all sides of meat. Add onions, garlic, Worcestershire sauce, bay leaf, oregano, salt, and pepper. Simmer, covered, 1½–2 hours or until meat is tender. Add vegetables. Cook until vegetables are tender, 30–45 minutes. Mix flour and water; stir mixture into stew. Cook and stir stew until thickened and bubbly. If you would like additional color, add browning sauce. Remove and discard bay leaf. Serve.

POT ROAST WITH SPAGHETTI

2 tablespoons cooking oil
2 tablespoons butter
1 chuck roast, 2–3 pounds
1 garlic clove, minced
1 small onion, chopped
2 teaspoons dried oregano
1 teaspoon dried thyme
$\frac{1}{2}$ teaspoon dried basil
$\frac{1}{8}$ teaspoon ground cinnamon
$1\frac{1}{2}$–2 teaspoons salt
$\frac{1}{2}$ teaspoon pepper
3 cups hot water
3 6-ounce cans tomato paste
1 pound spaghetti, cooked and drained
Grated Parmesan cheese (optional)

In a Dutch oven, heat oil and butter. Brown all sides of meat evenly. Remove meat and set aside. Add garlic, onion, and other seasonings to Dutch oven. Cook mixture slowly for 5 minutes, stirring continually. Add water and tomato paste; stir until well blended. Return roast to Dutch oven and spoon sauce over meat. Cover; simmer $2\frac{1}{2}$–3 hours or until roast is tender. Remove roast; slice. Serve with spaghetti and sauce. If desired, you may sprinkle with Parmesan cheese.

SWISS STEAK AND POTATOES

5 cups thinly sliced small red potatoes
1 large onion, chopped
1 small clove garlic, minced
1 pound beef top round steak, trim off all fat and
    diagonally cut into 1-inch strips
1 15-ounce can reduced-sodium tomato sauce
$\frac{1}{3}$ cup ketchup
1 tablespoon packed brown sugar
1 tablespoon cider vinegar
$\frac{1}{2}$ teaspoon dried thyme
$\frac{1}{4}$ teaspoon salt
$\frac{1}{8}$ teaspoon pepper
1 large bay leaf

Combine potatoes, onions, and garlic in a $2\frac{1}{2}$-quart microwave-safe casserole dish. Microwave on high power for 5–6 minutes or until potatoes are partially cooked. Stir after 3 minutes. Lightly coat a Dutch oven with nonstick cooking spray. Add meat. Sauté over medium heat until meat is browned. Stir in tomato sauce, ketchup, brown sugar, vinegar, thyme, salt, pepper, and bay leaf. Stir in the potato mixture. Bring to a boil; reduce heat. Cover and simmer for 25–30 minutes or until meat is tender. Remove and discard bay leaf. Serve immediately.

BEEF TIPS WITH NOODLES

1 can cream of mushroom soup
1 package onion soup mix
2 pounds lean chunks of stew meat cut into bite-
    sized pieces
1 cup lemon-lime soda
Cooked noodles or rice

Place meat in a 2-quart casserole dish. Pour soup and soup mix over meat. Add soda. Do not mix together or stir. Cover casserole and bake at 275° for 4 hours. Do not open oven door during cooking. Let stand 30 minutes before serving. Serve over cooked noodles. May also serve over rice if preferred.

45-MINUTE CASSEROLE

1 pound ground beef
1 large onion, chopped
1 can cream of celery soup
Small can sauerkraut
Tater tots

Brown ground beef and onion; drain. Put meat and onion in casserole dish. Pour soup over top. Drain and rinse sauerkraut; pour over mixture in casserole. Cover top with tater tots. Bake at 350° for 45 minutes.

CRANBERRY PORK ROAST

1 lean, boneless pork roast
1 can jellied cranberry sauce
½ cup cranberry juice

½ cup sugar
1 teaspoon dry mustard
⅛ teaspoon cloves

Place roast in Crock-Pot. Combine and pour remaining ingredients over roast. Cook on low 6–8 hours. Thicken juice with cornstarch. Makes terrific gravy for mashed potatoes.

BAKED HAM SLICE

1 cup water
¼ cup white vinegar
¼ cup ketchup
3 tablespoons brown sugar
1 tablespoon Worcestershire sauce
4½–4¾-inch thick smoked, fully cooked ham slice

Combine water, vinegar, ketchup, brown sugar, and Worcestershire sauce in a 13x9x2-inch baking dish. Add ham to dish and cover tightly. Refrigerate 2–4 hours. Let stand 30 minutes after removing from refrigerator. Cover; bake at 350° for 30–40 minutes or until thoroughly heated. Baste occasionally.

STUFFED HAM SLICE

2 cups soft breadcrumbs
½ cup raisins
½ cup chopped peanuts
2 tablespoons dark corn
   syrup

½ teaspoon dry mustard
¼ cup butter, melted
2 ½-inch thick ham slices
Whole cloves

Combine breadcrumbs, raisins, peanuts, corn syrup, mustard, and butter in large bowl. Mix well. Put 1 ham slice in baking dish. Spread with crumb mixture. Place second ham slice on top. Pierce fat of ham with cloves. Bake at 300° for 1 hour.

APPLE MUSTARD GLAZED HAM

1 cup apple jelly
1 tablespoon prepared mustard
1 tablespoon lemon juice
¼ teaspoon ground nutmeg
1 fully cooked bone-in ham (5–7 pounds)
Whole cloves
Spiced apple rings (optional)

Mix jelly, mustard, lemon juice, and nutmeg together in a saucepan. Bring to a boil, stirring continually. Remove from heat. With a knife, make ½-inch deep diamond shapes over the ham. Insert a whole clove in the center of each diamond. Place ham on rack in a shallow roasting pan. Bake, uncovered, at 325° for 2–2½ hours or until meat thermometer reads 140°. During last 30 minutes of baking, baste ham twice with glaze. Use apple rings as a garnish, if desired.

PORK CHOPS AND APPLES

4 5-ounce pork loin chops
  (³/₄-inch thick)
Salt and pepper to taste
¼ cup packed brown sugar
¼ cup apple juice

¼ cup soy sauce
2 tablespoons ketchup
1 tablespoon cornstarch
¼ teaspoon ground ginger
1 medium apple

Place pork chops in a 12x7½x2-inch baking dish. Season with salt and pepper. Bake at 350° for 30 minutes. While chops are baking, combine brown sugar, apple juice, soy sauce, ketchup, cornstarch, and ginger. Core apple and cut into ³/₄-inch rings. Turn chops and top each chop with an apple ring. Spoon some sauce over each chop. Return to oven and bake for 30 more minutes until chops are no longer pink. Baste with juices once. Any remaining sauce may be heated and served with chops.

FRUITY PORK CHOPS

6 loin pork chops
  (½-inch thick)
1 tablespoon butter
12 dried apricots
6 dried pitted prunes
1½ cups apple juice

1 tablespoon sugar
1 teaspoon salt
¼ teaspoon curry powder
2 tablespoons cornstarch
2 tablespoons cold water

Brown pork chops in butter for 2 minutes on each side. Arrange dried fruit over the pork chops. Mix juice, sugar, salt, and curry powder, and pour over fruit. Cover and simmer for 1 hour. Remove meat and fruit and keep warm. Meanwhile, combine remaining 2 ingredients. Stir until smooth. Add to pan juices. Bring to a boil. Cook and stir until thickened, about 2 minutes. Serve with meat and fruit.

CREAMY BAKED CHICKEN

1 can condensed creamy chicken-mushroom soup,
   undiluted
4 chicken legs, skin removed
1½ teaspoons dried thyme leaves
2 pounds sweet potatoes, peeled and cut into 2-
   inch chunks
3 cups frozen green peas

Spread soup over bottom of a Dutch oven. Add chicken legs.
Coat thoroughly with soup. Sprinkle thyme over chicken. Add
sweet potatoes. Bake at 350° for 50 minutes. Add peas; stir and
cover. Bake 10 minutes longer or until chicken is no longer pink
near the bone and the vegetables are tender.

ROASTED CHICKEN AND ROSEMARY

1 medium roasting chicken, giblets and neck
   removed
3 tablespoons extra-virgin olive oil
Salt and pepper to taste
3 whole garlic cloves, peeled
2 sprigs fresh rosemary

Rinse chicken; place in medium-sized roasting pan. Pat off
excess water with paper towel. Drizzle bird with olive oil. Rub
salt and pepper into skin. Put garlic and rosemary into the cavity of chicken, allowing 1 inch of rosemary to stick out. Bake at
325° for 1½ hours or until juices from chicken run clear.

HOLIDAY ROAST TURKEY
AND DRESSING

4 tablespoons butter or margarine
1 large yellow onion, chopped
5 cups crumbled corn bread
5 cups toasted fresh breadcrumbs
1 teaspoon baking powder
1 teaspoon poultry seasoning
$^{1}/_{4}$ teaspoon black pepper
$^{3}/_{4}$ cup low-sodium chicken broth
1 large egg, lightly beaten
1 fresh or frozen and thawed turkey (12 pounds)
1 tablespoon vegetable oil

In a medium-sized saucepan, melt the butter over medium heat. Add the onion and sauté for 5 minutes or until tender. Remove from the heat. In a large bowl, combine the corn bread, breadcrumbs, baking powder, poultry seasoning, and pepper. Stir in the onion-butter mixture. In a small bowl, whisk together broth and egg. Stir into the corn bread mixture. Toss to coat well. Preheat oven to 325°. Rinse turkey; drain and pat dry. Remove neck and giblets. Stuff and truss turkey. Place, breast-side-up, on a rack in a large roasting pan. Brush with oil. Insert roasting thermometer into turkey thigh without touching bone. Spoon remaining stuffing into a lightly greased 2-quart casserole; cover and refrigerate. Roast turkey for 3–3½ hours or until thermometer registers 180°, basting often. Cover with foil to prevent overbrowning, if necessary. When 30 minutes of baking time remain, add the casserole of stuffing to the oven, adding an additional 2–3 tablespoons chicken broth if stuffing is dry. Let turkey stand for 15–20 minutes before carving. Meanwhile, prepare desired gravy.

ROAST GOOSE
WITH CURRANT STUFFING

1 large yellow onion, chopped
1 large tart apple, chopped
¼ cup low-sodium chicken broth
6 cups toasted fresh breadcrumbs
½ cup currants or chopped raisins
¼ cup slivered almonds, toasted
¼ cup minced parsley
1 teaspoon dried sage leaves
¼ teaspoon each salt and black pepper
⅓ cup low-sodium chicken broth
1 goose (7–8 pounds), giblets removed

In a small saucepan, combine the onion, apple, and ¼ cup broth. Bring mixture to a boil. Reduce heat and simmer for 5 minutes or until onion and apple are tender. In a large mixing bowl, combine onion-apple mixture, breadcrumbs, currants, almonds, parsley, sage, salt, and pepper. Toss ⅓ cup broth with breadcrumb mixture. Preheat the oven to 350°. Rinse goose; drain and pat dry with towel. Prick the skin on the lower breast, legs, and around the wings with a skewer. Stuff and truss goose. Then place goose, breast side up, on a rack in large roasting pan. Insert a roasting thermometer into its thigh without touching bone. Spoon remaining stuffing into a lightly greased 1½-quart casserole; cover and refrigerate. Roast goose for 2–2½ hours or until the thermometer registers 175°, draining fat often. During the last 30 minutes of baking time, bake the covered casserole of stuffing alongside the goose. Let the goose stand for 15–20 minutes. Carve and discard the skin.

HERB-ROASTED ORANGE SALMON

2 tablespoons olive oil
¼ cup fresh orange juice
Finely grated zest of 1 orange
2 teaspoons minced garlic
2 teaspoons dried tarragon

Salt and coarsely ground
black pepper to taste
4 Salmon steaks (about 8
ounces each)
2 teaspoons freshly snipped
chives

In a large bowl, mix olive oil, orange juice, orange zest, garlic, tarragon, salt, and pepper. Place salmon in bowl with marinade. Let stand at room temperature for 1 hour, tossing occasionally. Place fully marinated salmon in baking dish and pour marinade over top. Bake at 475° for 7–8 minutes or until salmon is just cooked through. Turn and bake another 7–8 minutes. (Fish should flake easily when fork tested.) Remove fish to serving platter and sprinkle each steak with ½ teaspoon snipped chives.

BAKED HADDOCK

6 haddock fillets
1 teaspoon dill weed

3 medium lemons, sliced

TARTAR SAUCE

1 cup mayonnaise
¼ cup dill pickle relish
1 tablespoon sugar
1 tablespoon onion, finely chopped

1 tablespoon diced pimientos
1 teaspoon lemon juice
½ teaspoon dill weed

Grease a 15x10x1-inch baking pan. Arrange fillets in pan. Sprinkle with dill and top with lemon slices. Cover and bake at 350° for 30 minutes or until fish flakes easily. Meanwhile, combine remaining ingredients in a small serving bowl. Serve with hot fish.

MEATBALL LASAGNA

2 14½-ounce cans diced tomatoes, drained
1 8-ounce can tomato sauce
1 cup water
1 6-ounce can tomato paste
1 medium onion, chopped
1 garlic clove, minced
1 tablespoon dried basil
4 teaspoons dried parsley flakes
2 teaspoons sugar
Dash of garlic salt
8 uncooked lasagna noodles
24 cooked meatballs
1 egg
1 cup ricotta cheese
2 cups mozzarella cheese, shredded
¾ cup grated Parmesan cheese

Add first 10 ingredients to a large saucepan. Bring to a boil. Reduce to a simmer for 20 minutes. Cook noodles according to package directions. Drain noodles and set aside. Crumble meatballs into tomato mixture. In a separate bowl, mix the egg and ricotta cheese. Spoon 1 cup of meat sauce into a greased 13x9x2-inch dish. Top with 4 noodles, half of egg mixture, half of remaining meat sauce, and half of mozzarella and Parmesan cheeses. Repeat the layers. Cover and bake at 350° for 45 minutes. Uncover and bake 5–10 minutes longer or until light brown. Let stand 15 minutes.

CHEESY BEEF TETRAZZINI

1½ pounds ground beef, browned and drained
1 15-ounce can tomato sauce
½ teaspoon salt
¼ teaspoon pepper
1 8-ounce package cream cheese, softened
1 cup small-curd cottage cheese
1 cup sour cream
¼ cup green pepper, chopped
1 small onion, chopped
¼ cup thinly sliced green onion
1 8-ounce package thin spaghetti, cooked and
    drained
¼ cup grated Parmesan cheese

In a skillet, stir together cooked beef, tomato sauce, salt, and pepper. Bring to a boil. Reduce heat. Allow to simmer uncovered for 5 minutes. Meanwhile, beat cream cheese, cottage cheese, and sour cream until well blended. Add green pepper, onion, and spaghetti to cheese mixture. Transfer to a 1½-quart baking dish. Pour beef mixture over cheese mixture. Sprinkle with Parmesan cheese. Bake, uncovered, at 350° for 30–35 minutes.

*If desired, prepare casserole and refrigerate overnight. Bake right before serving.

QUICK AND
EASY DISHES

Progress in civilization has been accompanied by
progress in cookery.

FANNIE FARMER

BUSY-DAY CASSEROLE

5 blade steaks or boneless pork chops
2 large onions
4 medium potatoes
Carrots
1 8-ounce can low-sodium tomato sauce

Sear meat on each side. Place in baking dish. Cut onions in half and place on each piece of meat. Place potatoes around meat and then add carrots. Dilute tomato sauce with half water; pour over the meat and vegetables. Cover dish and bake at 350° for 2–2½ hours.

BEEF AND NOODLE CASSEROLE

1 pound ground beef
1 package noodles
1 can cream of mushroom
  soup
½ soup can milk
5 tablespoons butter
Salt and pepper to taste

Brown and drain ground beef. Cook noodles according to package directions; drain. Mix all ingredients in a casserole dish. Bake at 350° for 30 minutes.

EASY MEATLOAF

2 pounds uncooked ground
   beef
1 cup cracker crumbs
1 egg, lightly beaten
½ cup milk

1 teaspoon salt
¼ teaspoon pepper
½ cup chopped onion
¼ cup ketchup

Mix all ingredients. Form mixture into a large loaf. Bake at 350°
for 1 hour.

TATER TOT CASSEROLE

1 pound ground beef
1 can string beans, drained
1 can cream of mushroom soup
Tater tots
American cheese slices (optional)

Brown and drain beef. Mix with beans and mushroom soup.
Place in baking dish and top with tater tots. Bake at 300° until
tater tots turn brown. Top with American cheese slices, if
desired, and bake until cheese melts.

SOUPERBURGERS

1 pound ground beef
½ cup chopped onion
1 tablespoon shortening
1 can vegetarian vegetable soup
2 tablespoons ketchup
1 teaspoon prepared mustard
Dash of pepper
6 hamburger buns, toasted and buttered

Brown beef and onion in shortening. Stir to separate beef into small pieces. Add soup, ketchup, and seasonings. Simmer 5–10 minutes, allowing flavors to blend. Stir occasionally. Serve on toasted hamburger buns.

SLOPPY JOES

1 pound ground beef, browned
2 tablespoons minced onion
½ package onion soup mix
1 cup cheddar cheese, shredded
¼ cup ketchup
¼ cup water

Add all ingredients to skillet. Simmer 10 minutes and serve on buns. To freeze, place on buns and wrap with aluminum foil. When ready to use, unwrap and place on cookie sheet. Bake at 375° for 20 minutes.

QUICK AND EASY CHILI

1¼ pounds ground beef
1 large onion, chopped
1 16-ounce can whole tomatoes, undrained and
  chopped
1 16-ounce can pork and beans, undrained
1 15-ounce can kidney beans, undrained
1 11-ounce can zesty tomato soup, undiluted
2 tablespoons chili powder
1 teaspoon salt

Combine beef and onion in a Dutch oven. Brown mixture, stirring often, until meat is no longer pink and is separated into small pieces. Drain mixture. Add tomatoes and all remaining ingredients. Bring mixture to a boil. Cook 3 minutes, stirring occasionally.

BARBECUED BEEF

1 small green pepper, chopped
1 small onion, chopped
3 tablespoons shortening
1 12-ounce can corned beef
1 cup water
⅓ bottle ketchup
1 teaspoon cinnamon
⅛ teaspoon ground cloves
½ teaspoon Worcestershire sauce (optional)

Sauté pepper and onion in shortening. Add remaining ingredients to vegetables in skillet. Simmer 30–45 minutes. Refrigerate and serve later, if desired.

PIZZA CRESCENT BAKE

2 tubes refrigerated crescent
  rolls
1½ pounds ground beef

1 15-ounce can pizza sauce
2 cups cheese, shredded

Unroll 1 tube of crescent rolls. Place in a lightly greased 13x9x2-inch baking dish. Press rolls to seal perforations. Brown and drain beef. Sprinkle over dough. Top with sauce and cheese. Unroll remaining tube of rolls. Place over cheese; seal perforations. Bake at 350° for 30 minutes or until golden brown.

PARTY PIZZAS

1 can chopped black olives
1 can bacon bits
1 cup cheddar cheese, shredded

1 cup mayonnaise
2 loaves party rye bread

Combine first 4 ingredients in bowl; mix well. Spread over bread. Bake at 350° for 10 minutes.

15-MINUTE CREAMY FETTUCCINE ALFREDO

1 8-ounce package cream cheese, cubed
½ cup margarine
¾ cup Parmesan cheese, grated
½ cup milk
8 ounces fettuccine pasta, cooked and drained

In a large saucepan, stir together first 4 ingredients. Cook over low heat until smooth. Add pasta; toss lightly. If desired, add 1 cup frozen peas, thawed, and 1 cup cubed ham.

QUICK AND EASY ENCHILADAS

1 10-ounce can Swanson premium chicken
1 24-ounce jar salsa
2 cups taco cheese, shredded
8 flour tortillas

Drain and shred chicken. Mix with 1 cup of cheese and 1½–2 cups salsa. Spoon ¼ cup of mixture down the center of each tortilla; roll tortillas and place seam side down in an 11x7-inch baking dish. Evenly spread remaining salsa over tortillas. Sprinkle with remaining cheese. Bake at 350° for 30 minutes.

SUPER EASY
CHICKEN TETRAZZINI

¼ cup butter
1 can cream of mushroom
  soup
¼ teaspoon garlic salt
⅛ teaspoon pepper
2 chicken bouillon cubes
¼ cup water

8 ounces cooked spaghetti,
  drained
8 ounces cooked chicken,
  cubed
2 ounces Parmesan cheese,
  shredded

Melt butter in large skillet. Add soup, garlic salt, pepper, bouillon, and water. Bring mixture to a boil, stirring constantly. Add spaghetti and chicken; stir gently but completely. Pour mixture into casserole dish. Sprinkle with shredded cheese. Cover dish and bake at 400° for 20 minutes.

CHICKEN MOZZARELLA
SANDWICHES

4 frozen chicken breast patties
1 small jar spaghetti sauce
4 Kaiser rolls
1 cup mozzarella cheese, shredded

Cook chicken patties according to package directions. Meanwhile, heat spaghetti sauce. When patties are done, place on Kaiser rolls. Spread 1–2 tablespoons spaghetti sauce on each patty. Sprinkle with mozzarella cheese and cover with top half of roll.

CREAMED CHICKEN SANDWICHES

1 large can shredded chicken, drained
1 can cream of chicken soup, undiluted
Hamburger buns

Mix chicken and soup in saucepan. Heat thoroughly, stirring often. Serve on hamburger buns. Freezes well.

TURKEY ROLLS

2 boxes chicken-flavored Stove Top dressing
1½ pounds medium-sliced turkey breast
1 can cream of chicken soup, undiluted
1 cup milk

Prepare dressing according to package directions. Wrap turkey slices around a couple spoonfuls of dressing. Place seam side down in baking dish. Combine soup and milk; pour over turkey rolls. Bake at 350° for 20 minutes.

TUNA MELTS

2 ounces tuna, drained
2 tablespoons finely chopped onions
2 tablespoons finely chopped green peppers
1 egg, hard boiled
2–4 tablespoons mayonnaise
1 tablespoon prepared mustard
2 English muffins, split
2 slices American cheese, cut into thin strips

Combine all ingredients except cheese and muffins. Spread on muffin halves. Top with cheese strips. Broil 4–6 inches from heat for 1–2 minutes or until cheese is melted. Watch closely, as Tuna Melts will burn quickly.

GLAZED PORK CHOPS

6 pork chops
1 teaspoon salt
1½ cups brown sugar

3 tablespoons vinegar
1 tablespoon dry mustard
Dash ginger

Combine last 5 ingredients and spread over pork chops. Bake at 350° for 45–60 minutes, depending upon thickness of pork chops.

SWEDISH MEATBALLS AND NOODLES

1 12-ounce package egg noodles
½ of 38-ounce package frozen, cooked Swedish
   meatballs
1 10½-ounce jar brown mushroom gravy
1 cup sour cream
Dash nutmeg

Cook noodles according to package directions. Drain. Heat meatballs in the gravy. Gradually stir in sour cream and nutmeg. Serve over hot cooked noodles.

QUICK BEEF HASH

1 pound ground beef
1 medium onion, chopped
3 cups frozen hash browns, thawed
½ teaspoon salt
¼ teaspoon pepper
1 cup salsa
½ cup Co-Jack cheese, shredded
Sliced green onions and olives (optional)

Brown beef and onion over medium heat until meat is no longer pink. Drain. Add hash browns, salt, and pepper. Cook over medium heat until hash browns are lightly browned, about 7–9 minutes. Stir in salsa. Sprinkle cheese over top and cook until melted. If desired, garnish with onions and olives.

ORIENTAL NOODLES AND HAM

2 cups broccoli florets
1¾ cups water
1¼ cups fully cooked, cubed ham
1 tablespoon soy sauce
2 3-ounce packages oriental flavored Ramen
    noodles
Sliced olives (optional)

Mix broccoli, water, ham, and soy sauce in a large saucepan. Add one packet of noodle flavoring (other packet may be discarded). Break noodles into small pieces and add to broccoli mixture. Simmer until noodles are tender, about 6 minutes. Stir often. If desired, garnish with olives.

PARMESAN PASTA

8 ounces angel hair pasta
1 large tomato, chopped
1 3-ounce package sliced pepperoni
1 2¼-ounce can sliced olives, drained
¼ cup grated Parmesan cheese
3 tablespoons olive oil
½ teaspoon seasoned salt
¼ teaspoon garlic powder

Cook pasta according to package directions. Meanwhile, combine remaining ingredients in a large bowl. Drain cooked pasta and add to mixture in bowl. Toss to coat thoroughly.

HAMBURGER CASSEROLE

1 19-ounce can ready to serve chunky vegetable
    soup
1 pound ground beef, cooked and drained
1 6-ounce package stuffing mix
1/2 cup cheddar cheese, shredded

Stir soup into cooked beef. Set aside. Prepare stuffing mix according to directions on package. Spoon half of the stuffing into a greased 2-quart casserole dish. Top with soup mixture, cheddar cheese, and remaining stuffing. Bake at 350° for 30–35 minutes.

FREEZER SLOPPY JOES

1 pound ground sausage
1 pound ground beef
1 medium onion, chopped
16 sandwich buns, split
2 8-ounce cans tomato sauce
2 tablespoons prepared
    mustard
1 teaspoon dried parsley
    flakes
1 teaspoon garlic powder
1 teaspoon salt
1/4 teaspoon pepper
1/4 teaspoon dried oregano

Brown sausage, beef, and onion until meat is completely cooked. Drain. Scoop centers from top and bottom of each bun. Tear removed bread into chunks. Add to meat mixture. Stir remaining ingredients into meat mixture. Put 1/3 cup of meat mixture onto the bottom of each bun. Cover with tops of buns. Wrap each sandwich in heavy-duty aluminum foil. Bake at 350° for 20 minutes. If desired, freeze sloppy joes for up to 3 months. When ready to use, bake at 350° for 35 minutes or until heated through.

CREAMED TUNA SANDWICHES

1 can cream of chicken soup
1 6½-ounce can tuna, drained
2 tablespoons minced onion
1 tablespoon finely chopped green pepper
4 slices toast

Combine all ingredients except toast. Bring to a boil; reduce heat and simmer for 7–10 minutes or until vegetables are tender. Stir often while simmering. Spoon over toast and serve.

BARBECUED HAM HOAGIES

1 cup barbecue sauce
¾ teaspoon ground mustard
¾ teaspoon garlic salt
¼ teaspoon ground cloves
1 pound chip chop ham

Lettuce leaves
Sliced tomato (optional)
Sliced onion (optional)
Sliced Swiss cheese
6 hoagie buns, split

Combine barbecue sauce, ground mustard, garlic salt, cloves, and ham in a saucepan. Bring to a boil over medium heat. Reduce heat and cover. Simmer mixture for 15 minutes. Place lettuce, tomato, onion, and cheese on buns, and add heated ham mixture. If desired, make a larger batch for a party and keep meat warm in a slow cooker.

MEXIMELT

1 pound ground beef, browned and drained
2 16-ounce jars salsa
1½ cups water
1 teaspoon chili powder
1½ cups uncooked rice
1 cup Monterey Jack cheese, shredded

Combine cooked beef, salsa, water, and chili powder in a skillet. Bring to a boil. Add rice to skillet. Cover and remove from heat. Let stand until all liquid is absorbed, 5–7 minutes. Fluff mixture with fork and sprinkle with cheese. Cover and let stand until cheese is melted, 2–3 minutes.

CRISPY CHICKEN

1 fryer chicken, cut up   ½ teaspoon seasoned salt
½ cup buttermilk   2 cups instant potatoes

Remove skin from chicken. In a bowl, mix buttermilk and seasoned salt. Dip chicken pieces in buttermilk mixture. Roll chicken pieces in instant potatoes, being sure to coat well. Bake at 375° for 1 hour or until chicken is done.

BACON-TOMATO MELTS

2 bagels, split and toasted
8 tomato slices
8 bacon strips, fried and
   drained

1 cup mozzarella cheese,
   shredded
Prepared ranch salad
   dressing

Place bagel halves, split side up, on a baking sheet. Place 2 tomato slices and 2 bacon strips on top of each bagel half. Sprinkle with cheese. Broil 5 inches from heat for 1–2 minutes or until cheese starts to melt. Watch carefully to prevent burning. Serve with ranch dressing if desired.

THANKSGIVING LEFTOVERS PIE

3 cups prepared stuffing
2 cups cubed cooked turkey
1 cup Swiss cheese, shredded

3 eggs
½ cup milk

Thoroughly grease a 9-inch pie plate. Press stuffing onto the bottom and up the sides of the pie plate. Add turkey and cheese. Beat together eggs and milk. Pour over cheese and turkey. Bake at 350° for 35–40 minutes or until fork inserted at the center comes out clean. Let stand briefly before cutting.

CORN AND CHICKEN WRAPS

2 cups cooked, cubed chicken breast
1 11-ounce can whole kernel corn, drained
1 cup salsa
1 cup cheddar cheese, shredded
8 6-inch flour tortillas, warmed

Combine chicken, corn, and salsa in a microwave-safe bowl. Cook until heated through. Sprinkle cheese over surface of tortillas and add ½ cup chicken mixture down the center of each tortilla. Roll tortillas and secure with toothpicks.

CLUB QUESADILLAS

½ cup mayonnaise
8 8-inch flour tortillas
4 lettuce leaves
2 medium tomatoes, sliced

8 slices deli turkey
8 slices deli ham
8 slices provolone cheese
8 bacon strips, cooked and drained
Salsa

Spread mayonnaise on each tortilla. Layer remaining ingredients, except salsa, on four of the tortillas. Top loaded tortillas with remaining tortillas. Cut into quarters and serve with salsa.

SOUPS
AND SALADS

He that sups upon salad goes not to bed fasting.

THOMAS FULLER

OLD-FASHIONED POTATO SOUP

8 medium-sized potatoes,
    peeled and cubed
1 quart milk
2 teaspoons salt
¼ teaspoon pepper

1 tablespoon butter
½ cup flour
1 egg, well beaten
2–4 tablespoons milk

In a large saucepan or Dutch oven, cook potatoes in boiling, salted water until tender; drain. Add 1 quart milk to potatoes and heat. Blend in salt and pepper. Stir regularly. Cut butter into flour; blend in egg and milk using only enough milk to make mixture thin enough to drop into hot soup. Drop large spoonfuls of mixture into soup. Cover and cook on low heat about 10 minutes. Stir occasionally to prevent scorching.

BACON-CHEDDAR POTATO SOUP

½ pound bacon
1 cup onion
½ cup celery, chopped
½ cup flour
1 tablespoon seasoned salt
1 teaspoon white pepper

2 cups chicken stock
2 cups milk
4 cups diced potatoes, cooked
1 cup sharp cheddar cheese
1 cup Velveeta cheese
1 cup heavy cream

In a medium stock pot, fry bacon until crisp and remove from fat. Add onions and celery and cook. Add flour and seasonings. Add chicken stock, milk, and potatoes. Bring to a boil, stirring constantly. Reduce heat and add cheese, stirring until cheese is completely melted. Stir in heavy cream. Serve soup with crumbled bacon on top.

CLAM CHOWDER

2 tablespoons butter
¼ cup chopped celery
2 tablespoons chopped onion

1 cup potatoes, cubed
1 cup milk
2 cups minced clams and juice

In melted butter, sauté celery and onions until brown. Add potatoes and cook until tender. Add milk and clams; heat thoroughly.

CROCK-POT CHILI

1 pound ground beef
1 medium yellow onion, diced
1 15¼-ounce can chili beans
1 packet chili seasoning mix
1 28-ounce can Italian-style diced tomatoes

Brown and drain ground beef and onion. Add all ingredients to a Crock-Pot. Cook on low for 2–4 hours.

EASY CHILI

1 pound ground beef
1 cup chopped onion
2 1-pound cans stewed
  tomatoes
2 1-pound cans kidney
  beans

2 tablespoons chili powder
1 teaspoon salt
2 tablespoons sugar
2 tablespoons vinegar
2 teaspoons garlic powder

Brown beef and onions in a large, heavy saucepan. When beef is done and onions are transparent, drain grease. Add remaining ingredients and simmer for 20 minutes.

DAD'S BEAN SOUP

1 pound pinto beans
1 smoked ham hock
1 pound ham

2 stalks celery
1 onion
3 or more carrots

Rinse beans and put in Dutch oven. Fill Dutch oven half full of water and add the ham hock. Cut ham into small chunks and add to Dutch oven. Dice celery, onion, and carrots, and add to mixture. Bring soup to boil, then lower heat. Cover and cook slowly for 2–2½ hours. Add more water if necessary.

BROCCOLI CHEESE SOUP

½ cup onions, chopped
¼ cup margarine
5 cups water
3 tablespoons chicken
  base

1 28-ounce package fine noodles
2 12-ounce packages frozen
  broccoli
5 cups milk
2 pounds Velveeta cheese

In a large pot, sauté onions in melted margarine. Add water, chicken base, and noodles. Cook until noodles are tender. Add broccoli and cook for 5 minutes. Add milk and Velveeta cheese. Cook about 1 hour or until cheese is melted.

BROCCOLI SOUP

1½ cups water
1 bunch broccoli, chopped
1 large stalk celery, chopped
2 tablespoons margarine
2 tablespoons flour
2 cups water

½ can cheddar cheese soup
1 tablespoon instant
  chicken bouillon
¾ teaspoon salt
⅛ teaspoon pepper
½ cup whipping cream

In a 3-quart saucepan, bring 1½ cups water to a boil. Add vegetables. Cover and cook until vegetables are tender, about 10 minutes. Do not drain. Press thoroughly with potato masher or put through a blender. Melt margarine in a 3-quart saucepan over low heat. Stir in flour. Cook until smooth and bubbly. Remove from heat. Add 2 cups water. Bring to boil, stirring constantly. Add cheese soup; stir until smooth. Add broccoli mixture, bouillon, salt, and pepper. Heat just to boiling. Stir in cream, but do not allow to boil.

VEGETABLE SOUP

3–4 pounds rump or boneless chuck roast
1 beef bouillon cube
1 large can tomatoes
1 small can tomatoes
1 medium can tomato juice
1 cup diced celery
1 large onion, diced
6–7 large potatoes, diced
1 cup chopped cabbage
1 cup sliced carrots
1 can yellow lima beans
1 can green lima beans
1 can green string beans
1 can corn
1 can peas
½ cup fine noodles

In a large kettle, add first 10 ingredients. Cover with water and cook for 2 hours. Add water as necessary. After 2 hours, add next 5 ingredients. Cook at 300° for 1–1½ hours, making sure vegetables don't get mushy. Turn off heat; add noodles. Stir completely and cover with lid for about 30 minutes or cook in oven on lowest heat setting.

CRANBERRY SALAD SUPREME

1 3-ounce package raspberry
  gelatin
1 cup boiling water
1 16-ounce can whole
  cranberry sauce
1 3-ounce package lemon
  gelatin
1 cup boiling water

1 3-ounce package cream
  cheese
⅓ cup mayonnaise
1 8-ounce can crushed
  pineapple
½ cup whipped cream
1 cup miniature
  marshmallows
2 tablespoons nuts, chopped

Dissolve raspberry gelatin in 1 cup boiling water. Stir in whole cranberry sauce. Turn into 9x9x2-inch baking dish. Chill until partially set. Dissolve lemon gelatin in 1 cup boiling water. Beat together cream cheese and mayonnaise; gradually add lemon gelatin. Stir in undrained pineapple. Chill until partially set. Whip cream; fold in lemon mixture and marshmallows. Spread on top cranberry layer. Top with chopped nuts. Chill until firmly set.

FROZEN CRANBERRY SALAD

2 3-ounce packages cream
  cheese, softened
2 tablespoons mayonnaise
  or salad dressing
2 cups whipped topping
2 tablespoons sugar
Pinch salt

1 8-ounce can crushed
  pineapple, drained
½ cup pecans or walnuts,
  chopped
2 cups flaked coconut
  (optional)
1 14-ounce can cranberry
  sauce, jelled

In medium bowl, blend cream cheese and salad dressing. Fold in whipped topping; set aside. In a large mixing bowl, combine sugar, salt, pineapple, nuts, coconut, and cranberry sauce. Gently combine with cream cheese mixture. Spread into 13x9x2-inch pan. Cover and freeze. Thaw 10–15 minutes before serving. Cut into squares.

CAROL'S CRANBERRY SALAD

2 bags cranberries, ground
2–3 cups sugar
1 cup walnuts, chopped
1 can crushed pineapple, drained
1 pound grapes, halved
1 bag mini marshmallows
1 quart whipping cream, whipped

Grind cranberries in food processor; add sugar. Let stand for 1 hour. Add remaining ingredients and mix well.

CHERRY CRANBERRY JELL-O SALAD

1 cup water (or syrup drained from pineapple)
2 3-ounce packages cherry gelatin
1 cup lemon-lime soda, chilled
1 1-pound can whole cranberry sauce
1 9-ounce can crushed pineapple, drained
1/2 cup celery, chopped
1/4 cup nuts, chopped

Heat water or syrup to boiling. Add to gelatin, stirring until dissolved. Add soda. Chill until syrupy. Fold in cranberry sauce, then add pineapple, celery, and nuts. Pour into a 5-cup mold and chill until firm.

SPICED CRANBERRY RING

2 3-ounce packages raspberry
   gelatin
$1/8$ teaspoon salt
2 cups boiling water
$1/4$ teaspoon cinnamon
Dash ground cloves

2 6-ounce cans whole
   cranberry sauce
1 cup apples, diced
$1/2$ cup celery, diced
$1/2$ cup walnuts, diced

Dissolve gelatin and salt in boiling water. Stir in cinnamon and cloves. Add cranberry sauce; fold in apples, celery, and walnuts. Pour into a 6-cup mold. Chill until firm (about 4 hours). Unmold and garnish. Peach, pear, and apricot halves make nice garnishes.

FROZEN FRUIT SALAD

2 ripe bananas
1 16-ounce can pineapple juice
2 tablespoons lemon juice
1 cup orange juice
$1/2$ cup mayonnaise or salad dressing
1 10-ounce can mandarin oranges, undrained
$1/4$ cup sugar
Iceberg lettuce

Combine in blender: bananas, pineapple juice, and lemon juice. Blend 1 minute on low speed until smooth. Add and whirl $1/2$ minute on low: orange juice, mayonnaise or salad dressing, oranges, and sugar. Freeze 4 hours in 6 6-ounce molds or 1 9x9x2-inch pan. When ready to serve, cut and place on a lettuce leaf. Use as a dessert or salad.

FRUIT SALAD

1 2-pound can chunk pineapple
7 tablespoons sugar
2 tablespoons flour
2 eggs, beaten
½ teaspoon prepared
  mustard

1 tablespoon butter
12 marshmallows, cut up
1 small jar maraschino
  cherries, halved
1–2 bananas, sliced

Drain pineapple juice into a saucepan. Add sugar, flour, eggs, and mustard. Boil over medium until thickened, stirring often to prevent scorching. When thickened, remove from heat and add butter. Cool. When cool, mix in pineapple, marshmallows, cherries, and bananas. Add bananas last to help retain color.

SWEET POTATO SALAD
AND PEANUT BUTTER DRESSING

SALAD:

3 cups cubed cooked sweet
  potatoes
¼ cup chopped dates or
  raisins

1 banana, sliced
1 8-ounce can pineapple
  chunks, drained,
  reserving liquid

DRESSING:

¼ cup mayonnaise
2 tablespoons peanut butter
2 tablespoons reserved pineapple liquid
¼ teaspoon hot pepper sauce

Gently combine all salad ingredients in a large bowl. In a separate bowl, stir together all dressing ingredients. Pour over salad mixture and stir gently.

TROPICAL FRUIT SALAD

¼ cup mayonnaise
1 tablespoon sugar
½ teaspoon lemon juice
Dash salt
½ cup whipping cream
1 large red apple, chopped
1 large yellow apple,
   chopped

1 large banana, sliced
1 cup celery, sliced
½ cup chopped walnuts
Lettuce
½ cup toasted flaked coconut
   (optional)
Unpeeled apple slices
   (optional)

Blend mayonnaise, sugar, lemon juice, and salt. Set aside. Whip cream to form soft peaks. Fold whipping cream into first mixture. Slowly stir in chopped apples, banana, celery, and walnuts. Chill. Meanwhile, line a salad bowl with lettuce. Add chilled fruit to bowl. If desired, garnish with coconut and apple slices.

RASPBERRY MANDARIN ORANGE JELL-O MOLD

2 large packages raspberry gelatin
2 cups boiling water
1 can applesauce
2 10-ounce boxes frozen raspberries with syrup,
   thawed
2 small cans mandarin oranges with juice

Dissolve gelatin in boiling water. Add applesauce; stir thoroughly. Stir in fruits. Pour into Jell-O mold or Bundt pan. Chill until set.

WALDORF SALAD

White grapes
2 cups apples, diced
1 cup celery, diced
½ cup nuts

¼ cup mayonnaise
1 tablespoon sugar
1 teaspoon lemon juice
½ cup Cool Whip

Mix grapes, apples, celery, and nuts. In a separate bowl, mix mayonnaise, sugar, and lemon juice. Add to fruit mixture. Fold in Cool Whip.

CHERRY WALDORF SALAD

1 3-ounce package cherry
    gelatin
Dash salt
1 cup boiling water
½ cup cold water

½ cup apples, diced
½ cup banana, diced
¼ cup celery, chopped
½ cup nuts, chopped
Whipped cream

Dissolve gelatin and salt in boiling water. Stir in cold water. Chill until partially firm. Gradually add remaining ingredients. Pour into an 8x8-inch pan and chill until firm. Top with whipped cream.

MAKE-AHEAD SALAD

1 large head lettuce
1 head cauliflower
1 chopped green pepper
1 chopped purple onion
1 10-ounce bag frozen peas
1 teaspoon sugar

1 16-ounce jar mayonnaise
2 cups cheddar cheese, shredded
1 pound thin sliced bacon,
    cooked, drained, and
    crumbled
5 hard-boiled eggs

In a large bowl, mix lettuce, cauliflower, green pepper, onion, and peas. In a separate bowl, mix sugar and mayonnaise. Spread on top of salad. Sprinkle cheese and bacon on top. Refrigerate 8 hours or overnight. Before serving, chop eggs and add to salad. Mix all ingredients thoroughly.

SEVEN-LAYER SALAD

1 pound bacon
½ cup sugar
2 cups Miracle Whip
1 medium head lettuce,
    chopped

½ cup celery, diced
1 small box frozen peas,
    uncooked
½ cup onion, chopped
4 ounces cheddar cheese,
    shredded

Cook bacon until crisp. Drain and crumble; set aside. Dissolve sugar in Miracle Whip; set aside. Place half of the lettuce in a salad bowl. Then, in layers, add ¼ cup celery, half box of peas, ¼ cup onion, half of the bacon, half of the sugar mixture, and 2 ounces cheese. Repeat the layers. Do not mix the ingredients. Cover and let stand in refrigerator for at least 4 hours.

SAUERKRAUT SALAD

1 large jar sauerkraut,
   drained thoroughly
1 cup diced celery

½ cup carrot, grated
½ cup onion, chopped
½ cup green pepper, chopped

DRESSING:

½ cup vegetable oil
½ cup apple vinegar

1 cup sugar

Heat dressing ingredients together. Meanwhile, combine all vegetables. Pour warm dressing over vegetables. Toss gently. Refrigerate 24 hours before serving. Stir well before serving.

CHEERFUL COLESLAW

½ cup vegetable oil
¾ cup sugar
¾ cup cider vinegar
1½ teaspoons crushed
   celery seeds
2 teaspoons dry mustard
½ teaspoon salt
¼ teaspoon black pepper

½ head green cabbage,
   shredded
½ head red cabbage, shredded
1 small red onion, peeled
   and thinly sliced
1 green pepper, thinly sliced
1 red pepper, thinly sliced

In a nonaluminum saucepan, combine oil, sugar, and vinegar. Bring to a boil over medium heat. Stir occasionally. Reduce heat and simmer 5 minutes. Add celery seeds, mustard, salt, and pepper. Remove from heat. Toss dressing with vegetables. Cover and chill for at least 4 hours, stirring occasionally.

BROCCOLI-CAULIFLOWER SALAD

1 small head cauliflower
1 small head broccoli
1 small package radishes
2–3 large carrots

2–3 stalks celery
1 jar button mushrooms
1 large bottle Italian
dressing

Rinse cauliflower and broccoli. Cut into bite-sized pieces. Put into plastic bowl that has a tight fitting lid. Slice radishes, carrots, and celery. Add to bowl. Cut mushrooms in half and add to bowl. Add ½–¾ bottle Italian dressing. Put cover on bowl and shake the salad mixture. Allow to marinate in the refrigerator overnight. The next day add more dressing, if desired.

BROCCOLI SALAD

1 head broccoli, chopped
1 small onion, chopped
5 slices bacon, fried crisp
3 hard-cooked eggs, chopped
¾ cup cheddar cheese, shredded
1 cup mayonnaise combined with ¼ cup sugar
2 teaspoons slivered almonds
2 teaspoons toasted soybeans (optional)

Combine all ingredients in a large bowl. Cover and chill until ready to serve.

TURKEY AND POTATO SALAD

2 cups turkey, cooked and diced
2 stalks celery, chopped
2/3 cup water chestnuts, diced
3 green onions, sliced
2 red potatoes, cooked and cut into cubes
2 tablespoons parsley flakes
2 teaspoons dill weed
1 cup low-fat plain yogurt (or light or fat-free
    mayonnaise)
Pepper to taste

Lightly mix the turkey, celery, water chestnuts, onions, potatoes, parsley, and dill. Stir in the yogurt or mayo. Add pepper as desired.

GERMAN POTATO SALAD

1/4 pound bacon, diced fine
4 cups diced, cooked potatoes
1/2 cup chopped onion
1/3 cup vinegar
1/3 cup water
1 teaspoon salt
1/8 teaspoon pepper
1/8 teaspoon Accent
    (monosodium glutamate)
1 teaspoon dry mustard
1 tablespoon sugar
1 tablespoon flour

Fry bacon. Add onion and cook until yellow. Stir in vinegar and water. In a separate dish, blend together seasonings, sugar, and flour. Combine bacon mixture and seasoning mixture. Add potatoes and mix thoroughly. Heat thoroughly. May be reheated later for ultimate flavor. If desired, garnish with slices of hard-cooked egg, crisp bacon, and chopped onions or parsley.

SHRIMP AND RICE SALAD

1 cup cleaned, cooked shrimp
3 cups cooked rice
1/4 cup celery, sliced
1/4 cup green olives, sliced
1/4 cup green pepper, chopped
1/4 cup pimiento, chopped
1/4 cup onion, minced

1/2 teaspoon salt
1/4 teaspoon pepper
3 tablespoons mayonnaise
Crisp greens
2 tomatoes cut into wedges
1/2 cup French dressing
1 lemon cut into wedges

Split each shrimp lengthwise. In a large bowl, mix shrimp and next 6 ingredients. Cover and refrigerate. When ready to serve, mix salt, pepper, and mayonnaise. Stir into shrimp mixture. Spoon shrimp mixture onto crisp greens and garnish with remaining ingredients.

CHICKEN SALAD

3 cups cubed, cooked
    chicken breast
1 cup celery
1/4 cup green pepper

2 teaspoons onion,
    chopped finely
2/3 cup walnuts
2 cups white seedless grapes

DRESSING:

1/4 cup half-and-half
1 teaspoon salt
1/8 teaspoon pepper

2 tablespoons white vinegar
2/3 cup Miracle Whip

Toss all salad ingredients together. Set aside. In a separate bowl, mix together dressing ingredients. Toss with salad. If desired, garnish with olives, parsley, or paprika.

TACO SALAD

1 pound ground beef
1 package taco seasoning
1 medium head lettuce, chopped
1 small can kidney beans

1 large onion, chopped
4 medium tomatoes, diced
8 ounces cheddar cheese, shredded
1 package Doritos, crushed

DRESSING:

8 ounces Thousand Island salad dressing

1 tablespoon taco seasoning
1 tablespoon taco sauce

Brown ground beef; drain. Add taco seasoning, reserving 1 tablespoon for dressing. Layer salad ingredients in a bowl starting with lettuce and ending with cheese. Do not add Doritos. Combine dressing ingredients. When ready to serve, toss salad with dressing and add crushed chips.

PASTA SALAD

1 pound twist pasta
8 ounces Italian dressing
8 ounces mozzarella cheese, shredded
1 jar green olives, sliced

1 cup red onion, chopped
1 cup celery, chopped
1 cup green pepper, diced
1 package pepperoni

Cook pasta until tender; drain and rinse. Combine all ingredients. Toss to be sure all ingredients are coated with dressing. Serve chilled.

VEGETABLES
AND SIDE DISHES

Let my words, like vegetables,
be tender and sweet,
for tomorrow I may have to eat them.

UNKNOWN

CLASSIC GREEN BEAN BAKE

1 10¾-ounce can cream of mushroom soup
½ cup milk
1 teaspoon soy sauce
Dash pepper
4 cups cut green beans, cooked
1 2.8-ounce can French-fried onions

Combine soup, milk, soy sauce, and pepper in a 1½-quart casserole dish. Stir in beans and half of the onions. Bake at 350° until hot (about 25 minutes). Stir the mixture and top with the remaining onions. Bake 5 minutes longer.

CREAMY GREEN BEANS

1 can cream of mushroom soup
3 16-ounce cans green beans
10 Fun Yuns

In a casserole dish, mix soup and beans. Top with Fun Yuns and bake at 350° for 40 minutes.

BAKED LIMAS IN SOUR CREAM

1 package dried lima beans
¾ cup butter, melted
1 pint sour cream

3 tablespoons maple syrup
3 teaspoons dry mustard
3 tablespoons onion, grated

Soak beans in water overnight. Parboil until half cooked. Drain beans. Put in a casserole dish and add other ingredients. Cover. Bake at 300° for 1 hour. Remove cover and bake for another hour. Watch to be sure the casserole does not become too dry. Add milk if needed.

SCALLOPED CORN

2 pints frozen corn, thawed
2 eggs
1 tablespoon margarine,
   melted

2 tablespoons flour
2 tablespoons sugar
½ teaspoon salt
Dash pepper

Mix all ingredients in a casserole dish. Bake at 325° for 1 hour.

ESCALLOPED
BROCCOLI AND CORN

15–16 ounces frozen broccoli cuts
1 1-pound can creamed corn
¼ cup Ritz cracker crumbs (8 crackers)
1 egg, beaten
2 tablespoons butter, melted
1 tablespoon onion, minced
½ teaspoon salt
Dash pepper
½ cup Ritz cracker crumbs mixed with 4 tablespoons melted butter

Combine first 8 ingredients in a 1½-quart casserole dish. Top
with buttered Ritz cracker crumbs. Bake at 350° for 45 minutes.

BROCCOLI AND RICE

2 10-ounce packages frozen chopped broccoli
2 cups cooked rice
1 teaspoon celery salt
3 cups cubed Velveeta cheese

Cook broccoli according to package directions. Drain completely.
Add rice and celery salt. Stir in Velveeta until melted and all
ingredients are completely mixed. Serve warm.

BROCCOLI CASSEROLE

½ cup butter
¼ cup onion
2 tablespoons flour
1 teaspoon salt
½ cup water

8 ounces Cheez Whiz
3 eggs, beaten
2 packages frozen chopped
  broccoli, thawed
½ cup cracker crumbs

Melt butter over low heat. Add onion. Then add flour, salt, and water. Stir mixture until smooth. Add the Cheez Whiz and eggs. Stir to form sauce. Mix broccoli with ¼ cup cracker crumbs. Pour sauce over broccoli mixture. Sprinkle ¼ cup cracker crumbs over broccoli. Bake at 350° for 45 minutes.

CHEESY BROCCOLI

1 package frozen chopped broccoli
½ cup mayonnaise
½ cup cream of mushroom soup, canned and
  undiluted
1 egg, beaten
1½ cups cheese, grated
1 cup crushed crackers

Cook broccoli according to package directions. Drain and cool completely. In a separate dish, combine mayonnaise, soup, egg, and cheese. Combine with cooled broccoli. Stir mixture completely and pour into a buttered baking dish. Sprinkle with cracker crumbs. Bake at 325° for 30 minutes.

CREAMY CARROTS

2–2½ pounds carrots, peeled and thinly sliced
1 tablespoon butter
2 teaspoons sugar
½ teaspoon salt
1 tablespoon flour
1 cup milk
Salt to taste
Pepper to taste
2 tablespoons parsley, minced

In a large saucepan, combine carrots, butter, sugar, and ½ teaspoon salt. Add enough water to cover mixture. Bring to a boil over high heat. Reduce heat and simmer for 15–20 minutes or until carrots are almost tender. With a slotted spoon, remove the carrots and set them aside. Over high heat, return liquid to a boil until it is reduced to a shiny glaze. Do not overcook or sugar will caramelize. Whisk flour into glaze and add milk. Constantly whisk until mixture returns to boil. Add salt and pepper to taste; reduce heat to a simmer and cook 2–3 minutes. Return carrots to pan and heat through. Just before serving, add parsley.

CHRISTMAS CARROTS

4 cups carrots, unpeeled
1 teaspoon salt

1 can cream of celery soup
$\frac{1}{4}$ cup stuffed olives

Cook carrots with skins on. Add salt. Allow to cool, then peel and slice the carrots. Place in a buttered casserole dish. Add cream of celery soup and stuffed olives. Cover and bake at 350° until bubbly. Uncover and cook 10 minutes longer.

BUTTERED CARROTS

1 cup water
$\frac{1}{4}$ teaspoon salt
6 medium carrots, julienned

2 tablespoons butter
1 tablespoon confectioners'
  sugar
$\frac{1}{2}$ teaspoon dried mint

Bring water and salt to a boil in a saucepan. Add carrots to water and cook until carrots are just tender, about 8 minutes. Drain and set aside. Melt butter in the same saucepan. Add confectioners' sugar and mint, stirring until well blended. Return carrots to pan. Cook and stir 2 minutes longer or until carrots are tender and well coated with butter mixture.

CAULIFLOWER
WITH CHEESE SAUCE

2 tablespoons butter
2 tablespoons flour
1/4 teaspoon salt
1/8 teaspoon pepper
1 cup milk

1/2 cup cheddar cheese, cubed
2 10-ounce packages frozen cauliflower

In a heavy saucepan, melt butter over low heat. Blend in flour and seasonings. Cook over low heat, stirring until mixture is smooth and bubbly. Remove from heat. Stir in milk. Bring to boil, stirring constantly. Boil one minute. Add cheese and stir until melted and well blended. Set aside. Cook cauliflower according to package directions. Drain. Pour cheese sauce over cauliflower.

WINTER VEGETABLES

1/2 pound fresh Brussels sprouts, halved
1/2 pound parsnips, peeled and cubed
1/2 pound fresh baby carrots
1 medium sweet potato, peeled and cubed
2 medium red potatoes, diced
2 medium white potatoes, peeled and diced
1/2 cup butter, melted
1 1/2 teaspoons rubbed sage
2 garlic cloves, minced

Grease a 13x9x2-inch baking dish. Combine vegetables and put them in dish. In a separate dish, stir together butter, sage, and garlic. Drizzle over vegetable mixture. Cover with aluminum foil and bake at 375° until vegetables are tender, about 45 minutes.

MIXED VEGETABLES
WITH SAUCE

³/₄ cup mayonnaise
1 small onion, diced
¹/₂ tablespoon Worcestershire sauce
2 hard-boiled eggs, diced
1 tablespoon cooking oil
¹/₂ tablespoon prepared mustard
1 small can water chestnuts, sliced
1 20-ounce bag frozen mixed vegetables

Mix all ingredients except mixed vegetables. Set aside. Cook frozen vegetables about 15 minutes or until barely done. Drain. Add sauce. Serve immediately or refrigerate and use as a salad.

CHEESY VEGETABLE
CASSEROLE

2 medium zucchini, quartered and sliced
2 medium tomatoes, diced
1 small onion, chopped
1 teaspoon Italian seasoning
1 teaspoon salt
¹/₂ teaspoon pepper
1¹/₂ cups mozzarella cheese, shredded

Combine vegetables in a 2-quart microwave-safe dish. Cover and microwave until vegetables are tender, about 13 minutes. Stir three times during cooking. When vegetables are tender, drain juices and sprinkle with seasonings and cheese. Cover and let stand until cheese is melted, about 3 minutes.

MEDLEY OF VEGETABLES

1 cup onions, chopped
2 cups celery, diced
2 cups carrots, sliced
2 cups green beans
   (fresh or canned)
2 cups tomatoes

1 cup green pepper, diced
1 tablespoon sugar
1 teaspoon salt
3 tablespoons tapioca
4 tablespoons butter

Mix all ingredients in a casserole dish. Cover. Bake at 350° for 2 hours.

BACON CHEESE POTATOES

$2\frac{1}{2}$–3 pounds potatoes
$\frac{1}{2}$ cup onion, finely chopped
1 pound American cheese, cubed
1 cup mayonnaise
$\frac{1}{2}$ pound sliced bacon, cooked and crumbled
$\frac{3}{4}$ cup ripe olives, sliced

Cook potatoes until tender. Cut into cubes. Put potatoes in a bowl and add onions, cheese, and mayonnaise. Transfer mixture to a 13x9x2-inch baking dish. Sprinkle bacon and olives over mixture. Bake at 350° for 35 minutes.

DENVER POTATO PIE

6 eggs
½ teaspoon onion powder
½ teaspoon thyme leaves
¼ teaspoon salt
⅛ teaspoon pepper

3 cups frozen hash browns
4 ounces Swiss cheese, shredded
½ cup diced ham
½ cup chopped green pepper
1 tomato, thinly sliced

Combine eggs, onion powder, thyme, salt, and pepper in a medium-sized mixing bowl. Beat well. Stir in hash browns, cheese, ham, and green pepper. Pour into a generously greased 9-inch pie plate. Bake at 350° for 40–45 minutes or until set. Garnish with tomato slices.

HERBED POTATOES

½ cup olive oil
¼ cup butter, melted
1 package onion soup mix
1 teaspoon dried thyme
1 teaspoon dried marjoram

¼ teaspoon pepper
2 pounds red potatoes,
   quartered
Minced fresh parsley (optional)

In a shallow dish, combine olive oil, butter, onion soup mix, thyme, marjoram, and pepper. Add potatoes two at a time. Coat potatoes with oil mixture. Place in a single layer in a greased 15x10x1-inch pan. Drizzle with remaining coating mixture. Bake at 450° for 50 minutes. Stir 4 times during baking. Sprinkle with fresh parsley if desired.

REFRIGERATOR MASHED POTATOES

5 pounds potatoes
4 cups water
2 teaspoons salt
½ cup butter
2 3-ounce packages cream
   cheese, cubed

2 tablespoons fresh or
   dried chives
1 teaspoon salt
⅛ teaspoon pepper
1½–1¾ cups milk
Butter

Peel potatoes and cut into quarters. Place potatoes in a Dutch oven with 4 cups water and 2 teaspoons salt. Heat over high heat until mixture boils. Reduce heat to low and cook until potatoes are tender. Drain. Mash potatoes until smooth. Add ½ cup butter, cream cheese, chives, salt, and pepper. Gradually add enough milk to make potatoes creamy and fluffy; mix well after each addition. Refrigerate in a tightly covered container for up to 2 weeks. For 6–8 servings, spread half of the potato mixture in a greased 8-inch glass baking dish. Dot with butter. Bake at 350° for 45 minutes. Potatoes may also be baked in a microwave oven for 10 minutes. Rotate dish one quarter turn after 5 minutes.

BAKED SWEET POTATOES

6–8 large sweet potatoes
Butter

Cinnamon (optional)

Wash potatoes. Cut ends and scars off. Wrap each potato in aluminum foil. Place loosely on cookie sheet. Bake at 425° for 45 minutes or until fork passes easily through. Unwrap potatoes. Butter generously. Sprinkle with cinnamon, if desired. Refrigerate any leftovers and rewarm when needed.

APPLE MALLOW YAM YUMS

$\frac{1}{2}$ teaspoon cinnamon
$\frac{1}{2}$ cup brown sugar
2 apples, peeled and sliced
$\frac{1}{3}$ cup chopped pecans

2 17-ounce cans yams, drained
$\frac{1}{4}$ cup margarine
2 cups miniature marshmallows

Combine cinnamon and brown sugar in a medium-sized mixing bowl. Toss apples and nuts with brown sugar mixture. Alternate layers of apples and yams in a 1$\frac{1}{2}$-quart casserole dish. Dot with margarine. Cover. Bake at 350° for 35–40 minutes. Sprinkle marshmallows over yams and apples. Broil until lightly browned.

CRANBERRY-APPLE SWEET POTATOES

5–6 medium sweet potatoes, peeled, or 2 18-ounce
    cans sweet potatoes
1 21-ounce can apple pie filling
1 8-ounce can whole cranberry sauce
2 tablespoons apricot preserves
2 tablespoons orange marmalade

If using fresh potatoes, cut sweet potatoes into bite-sized pieces. Put in a large saucepan. Cover in salted water. Bring to a boil. Boil until tender. Drain and set aside. If using canned sweet potatoes, drain and cut potatoes into bite-sized pieces. Set aside. Spread pie filling in an 8x8x2-inch baking dish. Arrange sweet potato pieces on top of the pie filling. In a mixing bowl, stir together the cranberry sauce, apricot preserves, and orange marmalade. Spread sauce mixture over sweet potatoes. Bake, uncovered, at 350° for 20–25 minutes or until heated through.

SWEET POTATO DELIGHT

2 large cans sweet potatoes
1 large can chunk pineapple, drained with juice
    reserved

SYRUP:

1 cup brown sugar   3 tablespoons cornstarch
3 tablespoons butter   Reserved pineapple juice

Combine syrup ingredients in a saucepan. Cook until clear. Set aside. Drain potatoes and cut into chunks. Place in a 13x9x2-inch baking dish. Top potatoes with pineapple chunks. Pour syrup over top. Bake at 350° for 35 minutes.

GLAZED BUTTERNUT SQUASH

2½ pounds butternut squash
½ cup packed brown sugar
¼ cup butter

¼ teaspoon paprika
½ teaspoon salt
Dash pepper

Slice squash into 1-inch slices. Remove seeds and place squash slices on the bottom of a 13x9x2-inch baking dish. Cover and bake at 350° for 1 hour. Meanwhile, combine remaining ingredients in a saucepan. Cook and stir until bubbly. Drizzle over baked squash. Return dish, uncovered, to oven and bake 25 minutes longer, or until squash is tender.

BAKED ACORN SQUASH

3 medium acorn squash
¼ cup butter
¼ teaspoon cinnamon

½ teaspoon salt
¼ teaspoon ginger
⅓ cup honey

Cut squash lengthwise. Place in a 13x9x2-inch baking dish, cut side down. Pour ½ inch water over squash. Bake at 375° for 1 hour. Meanwhile, combine remaining ingredients. When squash is done baking, pour off water. Turn slices over and drizzle with sauce. Return to oven and bake 15 minutes longer.

MUSHROOM PECAN RICE

1 cup brown rice, uncooked
½ teaspoon ground nutmeg
1 10¾-ounce can cream of mushroom soup,
     undiluted
1 4-ounce can mushroom stems and pieces,
     drained
½ cup coarsely chopped pecans
2 tablespoons butter, melted

Cook rice according to package directions. Combine rice with nutmeg, mushroom soup, and mushroom pieces. Put mixture into a greased 2-quart baking dish; set aside. Sauté pecans in butter until they are lightly toasted. Sprinkle over rice mixture. Bake at 350° for 20 minutes.

WILD RICE AND APPLES

2 teaspoons olive oil
4 shallots, minced
4 garlic cloves, minced
3 cups instant wild or
     brown rice
3 cups ready-to-serve
     chicken broth
2 cups chopped apples
¼ teaspoon pepper
¼ cup chopped fresh parsley

Using a nonstick saucepan, heat oil over medium heat. When oil is hot, add shallots and garlic. Cook and stir for 1 minute. Gradually add rice, broth, apples, and pepper. Bring to a boil. Reduce heat to low. Cover and cook until rice is tender, 10–15 minutes. Remove from heat. Let stand 5 minutes. Drain any liquid. Stir in parsley.

CHICKEN AND NOODLES

5½ cups chicken broth
2 chicken bouillon cubes
½ small onion, minced
2 5-ounce cans chicken
1 teaspoon parsley flakes
1 12-ounce package frozen egg noodles

In a large saucepan, combine broth, bouillon, onion, chicken, and parsley. Bring to a boil. Add frozen noodles, stirring to separate. Reduce to simmer. Simmer for 50 minutes. If extra color is desired, sprinkle mixture with ¼ teaspoon parsley just before serving.

CREAMY NOODLES

1 12-ounce package wide
   egg noodles
¼ cup butter, softened
½ cup evaporated milk

¼ cup Parmesan cheese
2¼ teaspoons Italian salad
   dressing mix

Cook noodles according to package directions. Drain. Toss noodles and butter together in a bowl. Add all other ingredients and mix thoroughly. Serve immediately.

TURKEY STUFFING

For a 6- to 8-pound turkey

⅔ cup shortening
¾ cup onion, chopped
1 cup celery, chopped
16–18 slices bread, cubed
2 teaspoons salt

½ teaspoon pepper
1 tablespoon poultry seasoning
1⅓ tablespoons parsley,
   chopped
1½ cups hot water

Melt shortening in skillet. Add onion and celery; sauté over low heat for 15 minutes. Pour mixture over bread cubes that have been mixed with salt, pepper, poultry seasoning, and parsley. Add hot water; mix thoroughly. Spoon stuffing into turkey, using just enough to fill. Because stuffing swells during roasting, pack it loosely. Bake extra stuffing in a casserole dish for the last 35–45 minutes of baking time.

SAVORY APPLE STUFFING

For an 8- to 10-pound turkey

1 large onion, chopped
½ cup celery, chopped
½ cup butter
3 cups chopped, peeled apples
½ cup raisins
2 tablespoons snipped parsley

1 teaspoon salt
½ teaspoon pepper
1 teaspoon dried sage,
   crushed
8 cups dried bread cubes
¼ cup chicken broth

In a large skillet, sauté onion and celery in butter until tender. Add apples, raisins, parsley, salt, pepper, and sage. Cover skillet and cook for 5 minutes. Toss vegetable mixture with bread cubes in a large bowl. Gradually add chicken broth and stir lightly. Fill turkey cavity lightly with stuffing and roast as directed. Remaining stuffing may be placed in a casserole dish and refrigerated until ready to bake. Bake beside turkey for last 35–45 minutes of roasting time.

INDEX

Beverages

BREADS

BREAKFAST DISHES

CAKES AND BARS

CANDIES

COOKIES

DESSERTS (MISCELLANEOUS)

MAIN DISHES

PIES

QUICK AND EASY DISHES